CREATIVE DESIGN

PAPER CRAFTS

CREATIVE DESIGN

PAPER CRAFTS

Cheryl Owen

a Salamander book

Published by Salamander Books Limited
LONDON • NEW YORK

Published by Salamander Books Ltd.,
129-137 York Way,
London N7 9LG,
United Kingdom.

© Salamander Books Ltd., 1991

ISBN 0 86101 573 8

Distributed by Hodder and Stoughton Services,
PO Box 6, Mill Road, Dunton Green,
Sevenoaks, Kent TN13 2XX

CREDITS

Craft Designs by: Cheryl Owen, Rosalind Burdett,
Annette Claxton, Suzie Major and Juliet Bawden
Editor-in-Chief: Jilly Glassborow
Designers: Kathy Gummer, Philip Gorton and Tony Truscott
Photographers: Steve Tanner and Terry Dilliway
Typeset by: Barbican Print and Marketing Services, London, and The Old Mill, London
Colour Separation by: Fotographics Ltd, London – Hong Kong, Scantrans Pte Ltd., Singapore
and Bantam Litho Ltd., England
Printed in Italy

CONTENTS

INTRODUCTION

Paper is a remarkably versatile material and rather underrated as a durable and exciting craft medium. It is available in a wide range of types, from flimsy gossamer tissue to tough practical cardboard, simple gummed squares to exquisite gift wrap. You will probably have a number of materials already to hand at home; but virtually all the items mentioned in this book are easy to obtain and relatively inexpensive to buy.

On the following pages we will help you transform paper and cardboard into a vast array of beautiful items. We have included unusual gift ideas: jewellery, pictures, picture frames, a lampshade and personalized stationery. There is also a section devoted to children's designs, where you will find ideas to brighten up kids' bedrooms, as well as projects which children can undertake themselves. Festive garlands, party pieces, table decorations, centrepieces and place settings are all included and there is a feast of ideas for creating your own greeting cards, wrapping paper and gift boxes.

Divided into chapters for easy access, each design is clearly explained and illustrated with step-by-step colour photographs. There are also a number of templates to help you with making boxes, or where free-hand drawing might prove difficult. Hopefully, this book is just the beginning and that you will find inspiration from the many suggestions included to create your own ideas and designs.

PAPER

If you look around your home you may be surprised to find how many suitable materials you already have from which to make your designs – materials such as left-over wrapping paper and wallpaper, or cardboard packets and boxes that can be cut up and re-used.

The range of papers available for paper crafts is endless and very inspiring. Apart from plain coloured papers available from art and craft shops, there is a wide variety of handmade papers and exotic gift wraps that will add a touch of sophistication to any design. Textured and flock papers are also available, adding a third dimension to collages.

Crepe paper is a very adaptable material because it stretches and comes in a wide range of colours. When cut against the grain, the cut edge can be gently stretched to give an attractive fluted edge.

CARDBOARD

Generally, where cardboard is required for a project, you should use thin, lightweight cardboard, roughly the same thickness as that used for cereal packets. Where thick cardboard has been suggested, it should be sturdy enough to crease when bent. Some cardboards have a thin coating on one side which has an attractive shiny, metallic or textured

Tissue paper and iridescent film, although delicate, can be used to stunning effect on mobiles or as a lining for handmade boxes and bowls. Paper doilies and pictures from greeting cards or magazines are perfect for making gift tags and greeting cards or to decorate boxes.

Brightly coloured gummed paper squares are easy to apply – you simply moisten the back and stick in position. This type of paper is very convenient when working on an intricate design.

CRAFT MATERIALS

finish. These are particularly good for making party hats and masks. Mounting board can be used for items that will be handled a lot. It is made up of layers of cardboard and comes in many thicknesses.

CRAFT ACCESSORIES

Even though you may wish to specialize in paper crafts, this shouldn't exclude using a wide range of other materials in conjunction with paper for that extra special effect. It is often the finishing touches that make a handmade item so special, and you will find craft shops are a treasure trove of suitable decorative objects – many of them very reasonably priced. Cotton pulp or polystyrene shapes are lightweight and suitable for decorating in many ways. Similarly, coloured pipecleaners, tiny pom-poms, stick on eyes, beads, sequins and jewellery components all add interest to a design.

Nowadays, there is an exciting range of Victorian scraps that are ideal for paper crafts, plus a wide variety of decorative sticky tapes that help give a professional finish to a project. Giftwrapping ribbons can also be used to great effect. They come in many colours and widths. The wide ribbons can be moistened so that they will stick to themselves and the narrow ribbons will coil attractively when pulled smoothly over the blade of a pair of scissors.

A wide range of different coloured and textured papers is available from art and craft shops, and the choice can be increased one hundred-fold if you also consider using wrapping paper or wallpaper for your designs. Giftwrapping ribbons, adhesive tapes, pipecleaners and pom-poms also come in a variety of bright colours and help add the finishing touches.

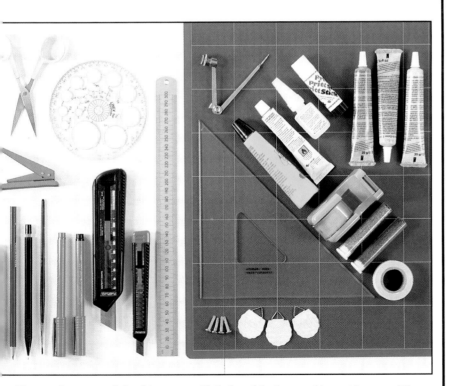

Here are just some of the things you will find useful when working with paper. They include a cutting mat, set square, steel rule, compass, craft knife and scissors, plus a range of pencils, pens, glues and tapes.

You may well find that you already have much of the basic equipment required for working with paper and cardboard at home. For best results, be sure to work on a clean, flat surface and, for safety, be sure not to leave any sharp implements lying around afterwards for children to find.

PENCILS AND DRAWING AIDS

An HB pencil is the most versatile pencil to use, but a softer lead such as 2B is better for sketching. Always keep pencils sharpened to a fine point so that your drawing is accurate. Be sure to use a ruler for drawing straight lines. A set square should be used for drawing squares and rectangles so that the angles are correct. Draw circles with a compass or, for tiny circles, use a plastic stencil.

SCISSORS AND KNIVES

A sharp, pointed pair of scissors is essential for working with paper. A small pair is more useful and easier to handle than a large pair. Craft knives give a better finish than scissors when cutting thick cardboard. Replace the blades frequently as they soon become blunt.

Always cut on a cutting mat – use a purpose-made mat or improvise, using a piece of corrugated cardboard. When cutting through thick cardboard, do not cut right through in one go but make several cuts, going deeper each time. Cut straight lines against a steel rule, preferably a safety one to protect your fingers. When cardboard needs to be folded, 'score' the surface lightly with a craft knife, being sure not to cut too deep into the board.

ADHESIVES AND TAPES

It is important to use the right glue for the job. Read the manufacturer's instructions carefully and test glues on scraps of paper first. When sticking thin papers together, make sure the glue does not seep through the paper. Also take care with printed papers as some glues will smudge the pattern. Use a plastic spreader or strip of cardboard to apply glue evenly over a flat surface.

For a professional finish use spray adhesive. Either put your work on newspaper spread over the work surface or place it inside a box to protect the surrounding area from spray. Spray an even film over the surface and then stick in place. The sprayed paper can be repositioned which is very useful, and any tacky areas can be cleaned up with lighter fuel. Always use an ozone-friendly spray adhesive and work in a well ventilated room.

PVA medium has many purposes. It is a non-toxic, white solution that does not stain, and is quite suitable for children to use. It can be used as a glue and to make papier-mâché. As it dries to a clear, glossy finish, it is also useful as a protective varnish.

Double-sided tape is sticky on both sides and provides a neater, cleaner alternative to glue. Clear sticky tape is very functional but remember that it does yellow and become brittle with age. An alternative is an opaque tape sometimes called magic or invisible tape which is longer-lasting but does not adhere so well.

Masking tape is a low-tack tape which is handy for holding paper and cardboard in place while you are working, and it does not leave a mark.

GIFTS & NOVELTIES

POTPOURRI CONE

Paper and cardboard can be quite tough and durable, so in this chapter we have included a number of clever ideas which make thoughtful and personal gifts for family and friends. Jewellery, personalized stationery and letter racks, pictures and picture frames, are just some of the many attractive items you can create. There is also a stylish lampshade, stunning Chinese lantern and a variety of designs to enhance ordinary trinket boxes. And this chapter also provides a selection of projects showing you how to create little novelty items such as gift cones and bon-bon baskets, ideal for dinner or party guests to take home with them.

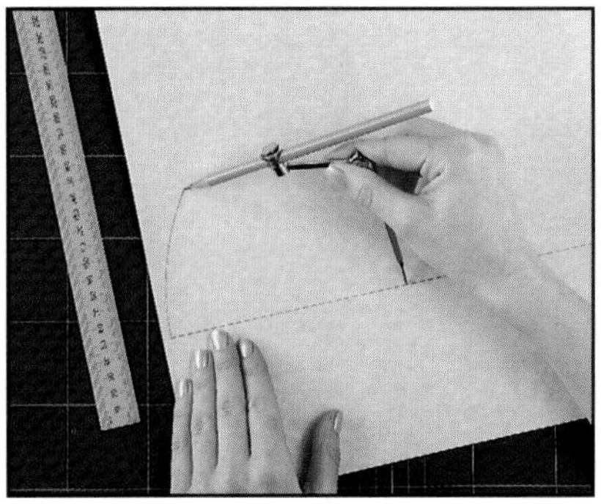

Fill this pretty cone with potpourri and allow the scent to waft through your home. Draw a 30cm (12in) diameter semi-circle with a compass on a piece of mottled peach-coloured paper. Cut it out and bend into the cone shape. Cut away a slice so the ends overlap smoothly and glue the overlapped ends together. Leave to dry.

Cut out motifs from a white paper doily and stick to the cone with spray glue. Coat the cone all over with PVA medium. Set aside until the medium has hardened and become clear and then apply two more coats.

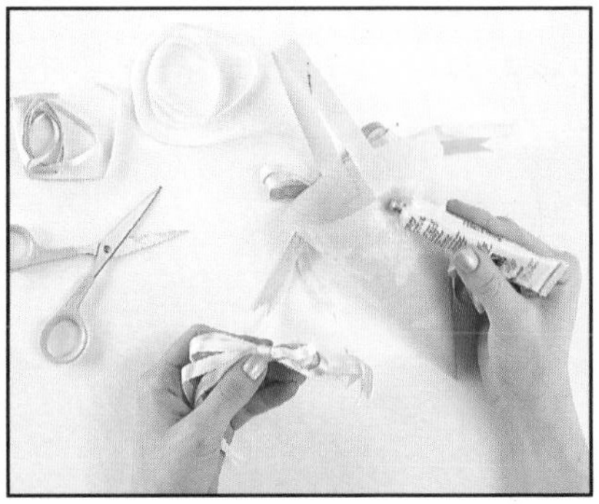

Cut a strip of paper 25cm x 1.5cm (10in x 5⁄8in) for the handle. Glue the ends inside the cone and coat with the PVA medium. Hang the handle over a door handle to dry. Tie ribbons in a bow and glue to the cone below the handle.

To make one of these pretty baskets you will need a sheet of paper 20cm (8in) square. Fold the square in half diagonally, then diagonally again. Place the triangle with the single fold running vertically. Bring the upper of the two free points up to meet the single point, opening the flap out as you do so to form a square. Crease the folds and repeat on the other side.

Position the newly formed square with the free edges pointing away from you. Fold the top free corner down to meet the opposite corner, then fold it back on itself to the horizontal centre line. Fold the flap in half once more. Repeat on the other side as shown. Turn the top left flap over to the right side, then fold it back on itself so that the corner meets the vertical centre line.

Fold the left hand corner in towards the vertical centre line also. Turn the basket over and repeat on the other side as shown. Open out the shape slightly and fold the top two flaps down inside the basket. Flatten the base. Cut a thin strip of paper for a handle and slip the ends into the slots on each side of the basket rim. Staple in place and decorate the basket with ribbons or lace.

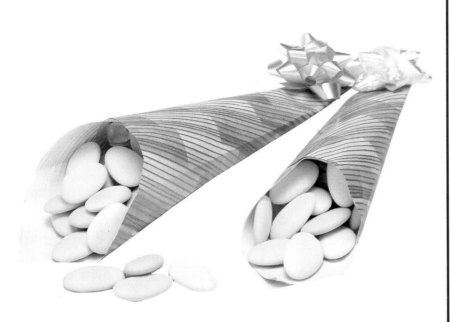

To make this simple gift for the table, fill a paper cone with chocolate drops or jellies for a children's party, or with sugared almonds for grown-ups. All you need is a small square of brightly coloured wrapping paper, a ribbon rosette, and some tissue paper. Simply roll the paper into a cone from corner to corner, taping it into a nice rounded shape.

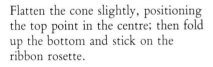

Flatten the cone slightly, positioning the top point in the centre; then fold up the bottom and stick on the ribbon rosette.

Scrunch up a little bit of tissue paper and slip it inside the cone to hold it in shape, then fill the top with sweets so that they spill out onto the point. You could attach a place card to each cone and use the cones to mark place settings at a large party.

Quilling is the traditional papercraft of making pictures from coiled paper strips. Cut coloured paper strips 4mm ($^3/_{16}$in) wide and about 20cm (8in) long. Scratch the end of a strip to soften the paper. Now coil the strip tightly between your thumb and finger. Release the coil so it springs open and glue the end against one side.

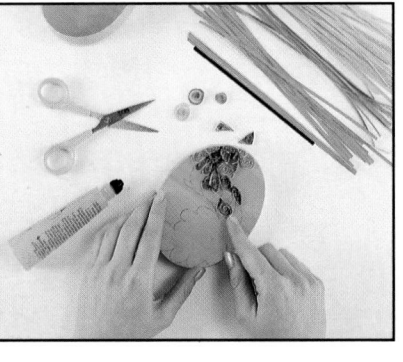

The coils can be gently squeezed into various shapes to fit your chosen design. Experiment with forming different shapes such as triangles and teardrops. To make smaller coils, cut shorter paper strips.

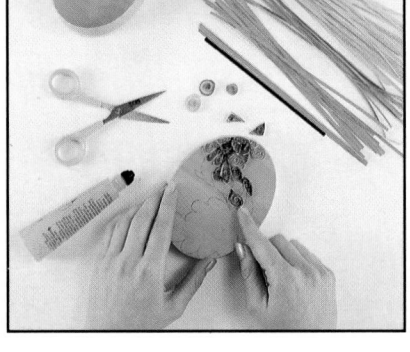

Draw a design on the lid of a wooden box and spread paper glue on a section of the lid. Arrange the coils on the glue and then move onto the next section. Fill in the whole design – any gaps around the motif can be filled with coils that match the colour of the box.

Transform ordinary pencils into these smart covered ones with scraps of wrapping paper. Choose round rather than hexagonal-shaped pencils. Cut a strip of wrapping paper wide enough to wrap around the pencil and as long as the pencil. Spray the back heavily with spray glue and wrap around the pencil.

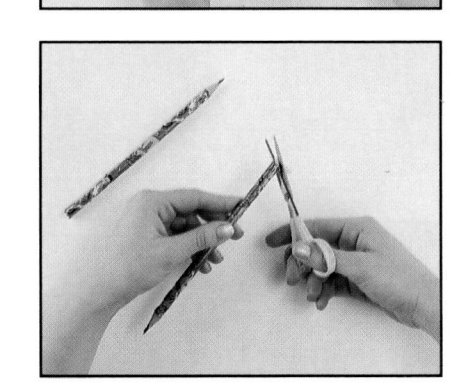

To finish, simply trim away the excess at the end of the pencil with a pair of small scissors.

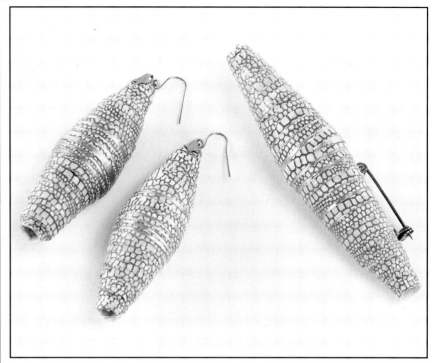

This bangle and matching necklace are made from papier–mâché. You will need suitable moulds for each – a small washing-up liquid bottle is the right size for the bangle and a garden stick is ideal for the beads. Cover the stick and 5cm (2in) at the end of the bottle with Vaseline. This stops the papier-mâché sticking to the mould.

Tear paper into small strips. Wallpaper lining paper was used for the bangle and newspaper for the necklace. Mix PVA medium (available at art shops) with a little water to thin it. Dip a brush in the solution, pick up a strip with the brush and press it onto the mould. Cover the Vaseline overlapping the strips. Apply four layers and leave to dry.

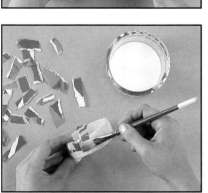

Build up the layers to about 5mm (¼in) thick and allow to dry overnight. Remove the jewellery, trim the bangle to 3cm (1¼in) wide with a craft knife and cut beads 3cm (1¼in) long. Tear giftwrap into small strips and apply to jewellery with the thinned PVA solution. Apply two coats of PVA medium as varnish. Thread beads onto cord.

No one will guess that this beautiful jewellery is made of paper. For each earring cut a long triangle of snakeskin-effect paper (available from specialist art shops) 76cm (30in) long with a 6cm (2¼in) wide base and gold giftwrap 75cm (29in) long with a 5cm (2in) wide base. Using PVA medium stick the giftwrap centrally to the wide end of the snakeskin piece.

Spread Vaseline on a length of wood dowel to stop the paper sticking to the wood. Starting at the wide end, roll the triangles tightly around the dowel, brushing with PVA medium as you go. Give the beads a final coat of the medium as a varnish, leave to dry, then gently remove the dowel.

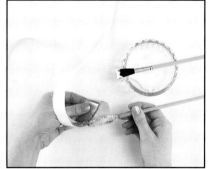

Pierce a hole through the top of each earring and attach a triangle wire. Fix a small jump ring to the triangle wire with a pair of pliers. Attach an earring hook to the ring. The brooch is made in the same way with wider triangles of snakeskin and gold paper. Glue a brooch pin to the back of the brooch. Craft shops sell jewellery components.

REGENCY SILHOUETTE

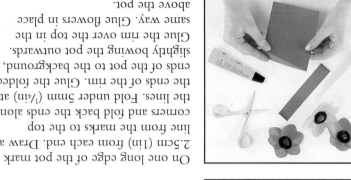

This delightful picture will brighten a dreary day. Cut a 3cm (1¼in) diameter circle of black paper; cut a fringe around the edge and a small hole in the centre. Cut a 6cm (2½in) diameter circle of black tissue paper and wrap it over a small ball of cotton wool (absorbent cotton). Twist the edges together and insert into the hole.

Use the template on page 25 to cut six petals from tissue paper and glue to the twisted end. Make two more flowers. Glue some striped wallpaper to a piece of cardboard and some cream paper over the lower third. From thick brown paper, cut a rectangle 13cm x 10cm (5in x 4in) for the pot and a strip 15cm x 2.5cm (6in x 1in) for the rim.

On one long edge of the pot mark 2.5cm (1in) from each end. Draw a line from the marks to the top corners and fold back the ends along the lines. Fold under 5mm (¼in) at the ends of the rim. Glue the folded ends of the pot to the background, slightly bowing the pot outwards. Glue the rim over the top in the same way. Glue flowers in place above the pot.

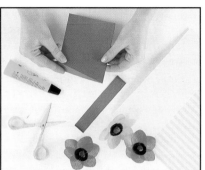

POT OF ANEMONES

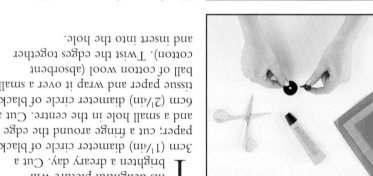

Give your home a period touch with this classic decoration. You can use a clear profile sketch or a photograph as a basis for your picture. Make a tracing of the outline and place it face down on the back of a piece of black paper. Redraw the design to transfer it.

Cut out the motif with a pair of small, sharp scissors and glue the design to white paper. Trim the paper to fit your frame. Place the picture in the frame and glue a small ribbon bow to the top.

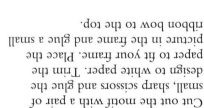

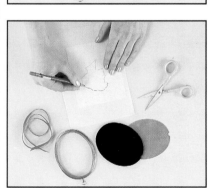

REGENCY SILHOUETTE

PHOTO FINISH

To make these smart frames, cut two pieces of mounting board 25cm x 19cm (10in x 7½in). Cut a window 17cm x 11cm (7in x 4½in) in the centre of one piece. Cut two pieces of giftwrap to cover the frames. Lay the window mount on the wrong side of one piece and cut a window in the giftwrap, leaving a 2cm (¾in) margin. Snip to the corners and glue the margins down.

Cover the back of the frame with giftwrap, then cut two 1cm (⅜in) wide strips of mounting board 18cm (7½in) long and one 22cm (8½in) long. Cover with paper and glue to the wrong side of the back just inside three of the edges. Spread glue on the strips and carefully place the front of the frame on top, checking that the outer edges are level.

Cut a rectangle of mounting board 18cm x 6cm (7½in x 2½in) for the stand. Score across the stand 5cm (2in) from one end. Cover the stand with giftwrap and glue the scored end to the back with the other end level with either a long or short side depending on whether your photo is in landscape or portrait form. Bend the stand outwards.

BORDERLINES

The right mount can really enhance a picture. Buy a plain cardboard mount to fit your picture. Draw a 1cm (⅜in) wide border around the window with a pencil. Cut four 1cm (⅜in) wide strips of marbled paper. Spray the back of one strip with spray glue and place on the border. Cut off the ends diagonally at the corners with a craft knife.

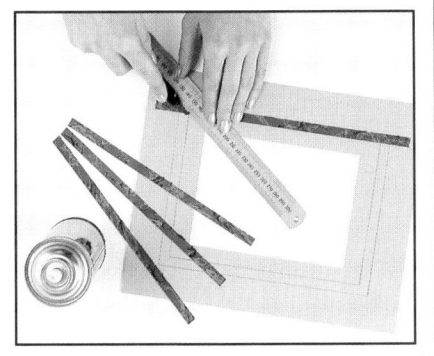

Apply the other strips to the mount, cutting the ends to meet diagonally in a mitred corner.

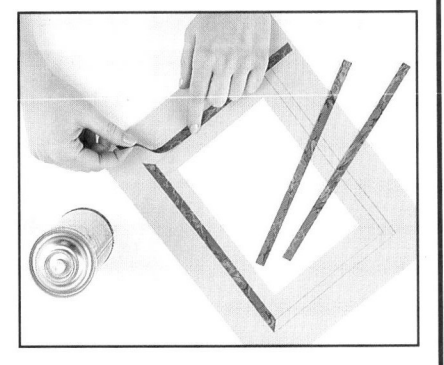

To complete the mount, draw a line each side of the border with a fine-tipped gold pen.

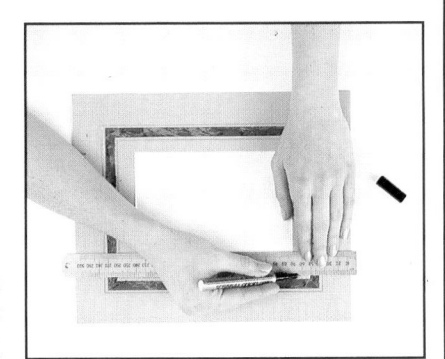

Drop two or three colours onto the water and swirl together with the end of a paint brush. Cut plain paper to fit the tray. Wearing rubber gloves, start at one end of the tray and lower the paper onto the surface of the water so it can pick up the pattern. Carefully lift up the paper.

Leave the paper to dry overnight on newspaper. You can remove the paint from the tray by drawing strips of newspaper across the surface of the water.

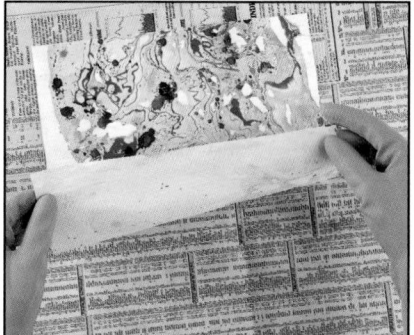

The marbled paper can be used in many ways. Here, a plain book takes on a sophisticated look when recovered. Cut a rectangle of marbled paper large enough to wrap around the book with a 2.5cm (1in) margin on all sides. Wrap the paper around the book, open the cover and glue the paper inside the opening edges.

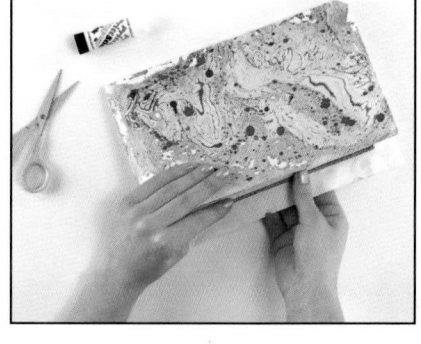

Prop up the book so the cover is open at a right angle. Snip the paper each side of the spine and stick the top and bottom margin inside the covers, folding under the corners.

There are many methods for marbling paper but this way needs little equipment. Fill a shallow tray with water. Put spots of enamel paint on the water with a paint brush. If they sink the paint is too thick and needs thinning with a little white spirit. If they disperse into a faint film it is too thin and should be mixed with more paint.

Push the paper at the ends of the spine between the spine and the pages with the points of a pair of scissors. Arrange jewellery stones on the cover and use a strong glue to stick them in place. Cut two pieces of paper to fit inside the covers and glue inside.

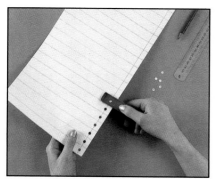

Co-ordinate your home with a pleated lampshade to match the wallpaper. For a 30cm (12in) wide shade cut a strip of wallpaper 130cm x 20cm (51in x 8in). On the wrong side, rule pleat lines across the strip 2cm (¾in) apart then draw a line along the length 1.2cm (½in) from the top. Punch a hole on this line between each pleat line.

Fold the strip in concertina pleats along the pleat lines. On the wrong side, slide each pleat into the punch in turn and make half a hole on the fold on the line. These holes will rest on the top section of the frame when the lampshade is finished.

Overlap the ends of the lampshade and thread ribbon through the holes in the middle of each pleat. Draw up the pleats and slip the lampshade over the frame, resting the notches on top of the frame. Pull the ribbon ends to tighten the top and tie in a decorative bow.

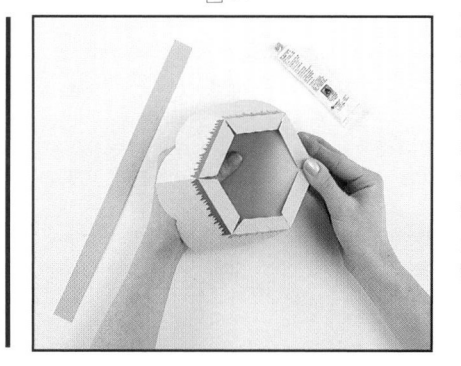

Fill this pretty basket with tiny sweet eggs to delight a child at Easter. Using the templates on page 25 cut out two sides and a base in pale blue cardboard and the grass in green gummed paper. Lightly score the sides of the basket along the broken lines with a craft knife, then stick on the grass.

Fold the sides backwards along the scored lines and join end to end in a ring by gluing each end tab under the opposite end of the other side. Glue the base under the base tabs. Cut a strip of pale blue cardboard for the handle measuring 30cm x 1cm (12in x ³/₈in). Stick the ends inside the basket.

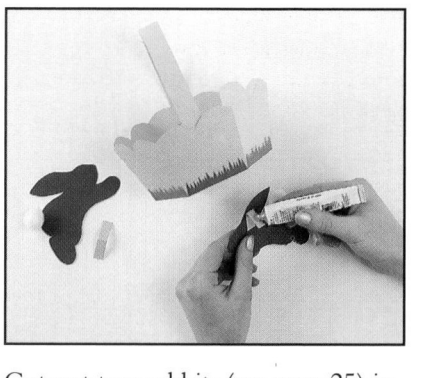

Cut out two rabbits (see page 25) in brown cardboard. Glue a ball of cotton wool (absorbent cotton) to the rabbits as bobtails. Cut two strips of pale blue cardboard 4cm x 1cm (1¹/₂in x ³/₈in) and fold them widthwise in half to make hinges. Glue one half to the back of the rabbit matching the fold to the broken line. Glue the other half to the basket under the handles.

FILIGREE STATIONERY

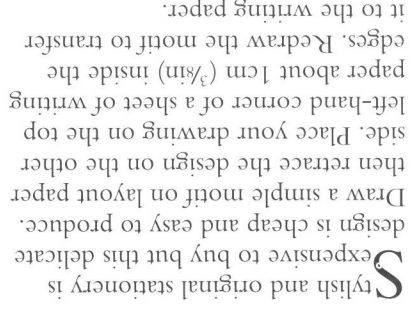

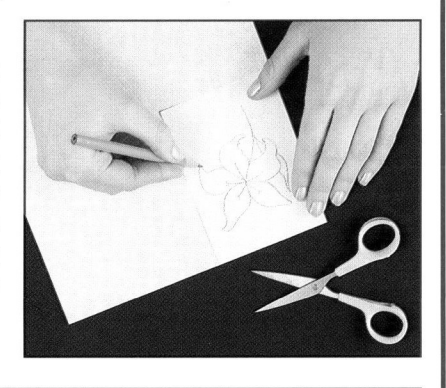

Stylish and original stationery is expensive to buy but this delicate design is cheap and easy to produce. Draw a simple motif on layout paper then retrace the design on the other side. Place your drawing on the top left-hand corner of a sheet of writing paper about 1cm (^{3}/$_8$in) inside the edges. Redraw the motif to transfer it to the writing paper.

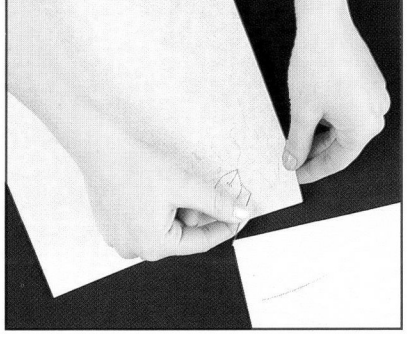

Now prick along the lines with a needle or pin. You may find it helpful to practise on a scrap of paper first to judge how far apart the pinpricks should be.

Rub out the pencil lines then trim away the corner of the paper to echo the shape of the design. Pinprick a co-ordinating motif on the matching envelope flap.

LETTER RACK

There is no excuse for mislaying letters with this smart letter rack. From thick mounting board cut a rectangle 24cm x 8cm (9½in x 3¼in) for the front and 24cm x 10cm (9½in x 4in) for the back. Diagonally trim away the top corners and cover one side of each piece with giftwrap.

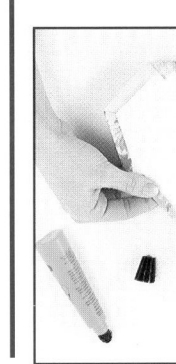

Cut giftwrap slightly smaller than the front and back sections and glue in position on the wrong side. Take a piece of wood 24cm (9½in) long by 3cm (1¼in) wide and 1cm (^{3}/$_8$in) thick. Cover the wood with coloured paper.

Cut a rectangle of mounting board 27cm x 7cm (10½in x 2¾in) for the base and cover with coloured paper. Use a strong glue to stick the front to one narrow edge of the wood keeping the lower edges level. Glue the back to the other side in the same way. Finish the letter rack by gluing this upper section centrally to the base.

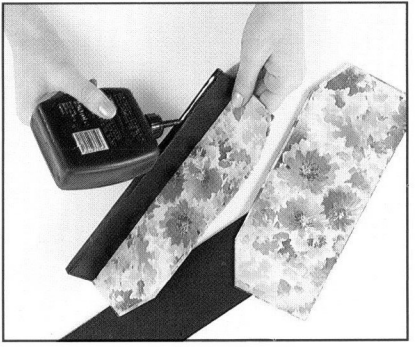

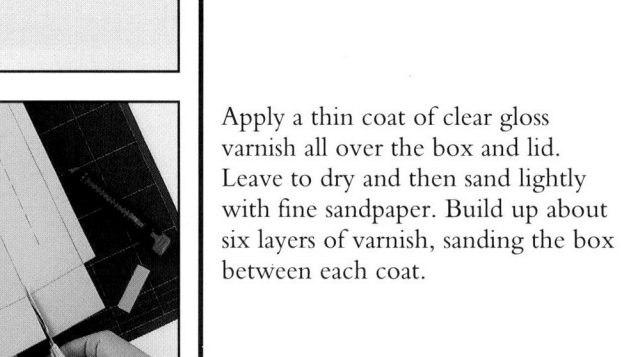

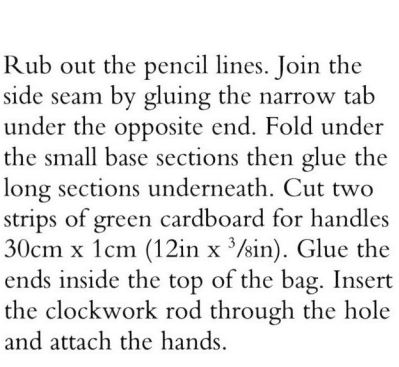

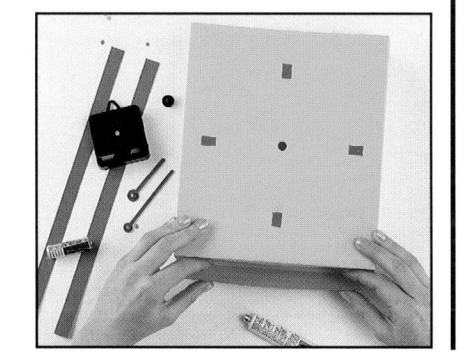

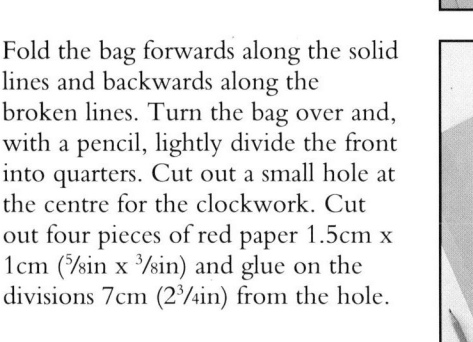

Make this carrier bag and you have a gift bag for your presents or go a step further and make the bag itself the present. Cut a piece of thick yellow cardboard 57.5cm x 29cm (22⅝in x 11½in). Refer to the diagram on page 25 and score along the solid and broken lines. Cut away the lower right-hand corner and cut into the base along the solid lines.

Fold the bag forwards along the solid lines and backwards along the broken lines. Turn the bag over and, with a pencil, lightly divide the front into quarters. Cut out a small hole at the centre for the clockwork. Cut out four pieces of red paper 1.5cm x 1cm (⅝in x ⅜in) and glue on the divisions 7cm (2¾in) from the hole.

Rub out the pencil lines. Join the side seam by gluing the narrow tab under the opposite end. Fold under the small base sections then glue the long sections underneath. Cut two strips of green cardboard for handles 30cm x 1cm (12in x ⅜in). Glue the ends inside the top of the bag. Insert the clockwork rod through the hole and attach the hands.

Revive the Victorian hobby of découpage and decorate a box with pretty paper pictures. Cut out suitable pictures from greeting cards or magazines or use reproductions of Victorian prints.

Arrange the pictures on the box and then stick them in place with spray glue. Smooth in place.

Apply a thin coat of clear gloss varnish all over the box and lid. Leave to dry and then sand lightly with fine sandpaper. Build up about six layers of varnish, sanding the box between each coat.

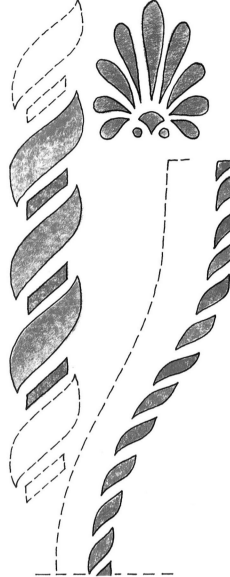

You could even decorate a simple DIY pine letter rack to match, for a lovely gift or a smart desk accessory. Sand the wood smooth and cut out two stencil sheets from the small curved rope design opposite. Tape the first stencil on to the wood and use quick-drying stencil paints, mixed up to match your decor, to stencil the first half of your design.

Match up the remainder of the design on the second stencil sheet and paint the second colour. Temporarily assemble the four walls of the letter rack with tape and stencil the large rope design (see above right) around the lower edge of the box in the same colours.

Above: Use these patterns to cut out your stencils for the letter rack and notepaper. The curved rope pattern only shows half of the design, so trace it off marking on the straight dotted centre line. Then turn the tracing over, match up the design, and trace in the other half accurately.

Hand painted notepaper and envelopes make a stylish and original gift. Use the stencils shown here to decorate the top of some sheets, working with oil-based stencil crayons. Rub a little crayon on to a corner of the stencil or a spare piece of acetate and then collect the colour on to a brush. Stencil the colour on to the paper using a circular movement.

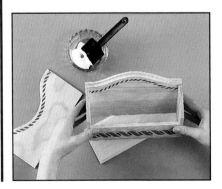

Decorate envelopes to match using the stencil crayons. Use a simple design along the lower edge or just a single motif that will not get in the way of the written address. Leave the stencilling to set for a while before using the notepaper and envelopes, to avoid smudging.

Now glue the box together using PVA wood glue. Begin with the four walls, then, when dry, glue these to the base. The centre section will then just slide into place. Glue this if you wish. Varnish the letter rack with several coats of clear polyurethane varnish to give a smooth, durable finish and to protect the stencilling.

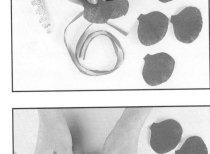

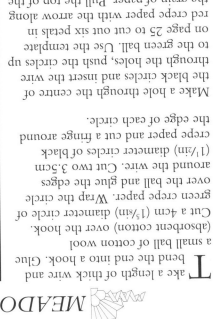

Take a length of thick wire and bend the end into a hook. Glue a small ball of cotton wool (absorbent cotton) over the hook. Cut a 4cm (1⅝in) diameter circle of green crepe paper. Wrap the circle over the ball and glue the edges around the wire. Cut two 3.5cm (1⅜in) diameter circles of black crepe paper and cut a fringe around the edge of each circle.

Make a hole through the centre of the black circles and insert the wire through the holes, push the circles up to the green ball. Use the template on page 25 to cut out six petals in red crepe paper. Pull the top of the petals between thumb and finger to flute the edges.

Glue the base of three petals under the poppy centre then glue the remaining petals in between. Bind the wire with a thin strip of green crepe paper and glue the ends in place to complete.

To make a daffodil, bend a 12cm (4¾in) length of thin wire in half for the stamen. Starting at the bent end, bind the wire with a narrow strip of yellow crepe paper. Secure the ends with a dab of glue. Cut yellow crepe paper 6cm x 4cm (2⅜in x 1⅝in) with the grain running along the short edges. Pull one long edge between thumb and finger to flute the edge.

Overlap the ends of the rectangle and glue together making the trumpet. Place the stamen in the trumpet and gather the lower edge tightly with thread. Using the template on page 25 cut six petals in yellow crepe paper with the grain running parallel with the arrow. Stretch the petals across their width.

Dab glue on the base of the petals and stick to the base of the trumpet. Place the stamen end and against a length of thick wire and bind together with a narrow strip of green crepe paper; glue the ends in place then bend the flowerhead forward. Fold strips of thick green paper in half lengthwise for leaves and cut pointed ends.

A zany idea for an unusual ornament or table centrepiece. For the apples fold a 12cm (4³⁄₄in) square of thin cardboard in half and draw half an apple shape against the fold. Cut out the apple then open out the cardboard to use as a template. Cut a total of 48 apples in light green and red tissue paper. Mix the colours and sew the pieces together along the centre.

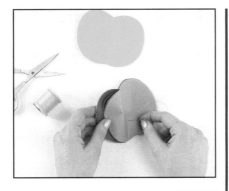

Lift up the apple halves on one side except the bottom one. Dab glue on the bottom half close to the edge in the centre and then each side between the centre and stitching. Press down the next half and dab glue close to the edge between the first positions. Continue to the top tissue layer, alternating positions.

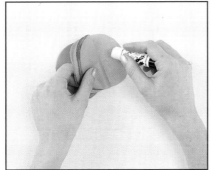

Glue the other half of the apple in the same way. Cut a stalk and leaf in green cardboard and glue to the top of the apple. Dab glue close to the edge in the centre and then either side between the centre and the stitching. Carefully press the two halves together and then glue the back halves together in the same way.

To make the carrots, draw a T shape on paper, the horizontal line 13cm (5in) long and the vertical line 20cm (8in) long. Join the lines together in a triangle. Cut out the triangle in orange crepe paper. Spread glue sparingly along one edge. Gently press the other long edge onto the glue and leave to dry.

Stuff the carrot with polyester filling, carefully pushing the filling in as far as possible with a knitting needle or skewer. Fold in the top edge for about 1cm (³⁄₈in).

Cut two strips of green crepe paper 10cm x 3cm (4in x 1¹⁄₄in), cutting the length along the grain. Roll the strips tightly lengthwise and glue along the long edges. Cut the strips in half. Hold the ends of these stalks inside the carrot and gather the folded edge tightly around the ends. Fasten the threads securely.

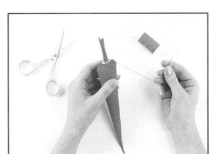

S tencil this attractive iris design on to thick watercolour paper for a linen texture and use wax stencil crayons for subtle colour shading. Size up the design and cut three stencils for mauve, yellow and green areas. Tape the green stencil in place and blend together two green crayons. Rub the crayons on to the acetate and then collect the colour on to the brush.

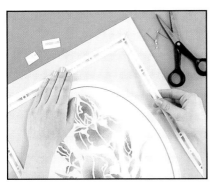

Remove the green stencil and tape the mauve one in position, lining up the vertical and horizontal marks. Blend mauve, blue and turquoise for the flowers, shading the lower petals in mauve and the upper ones in blues, and getting deeper towards the centre of each flower. Lastly, use the yellow stencil. Work the brush in a light circular motion to shade the colours throughout.

Have an oval mount cut to fit around your stencil. Cut out the border stencil from the design shown opposite and try it out on scrap paper in various colours. Cut these trial pieces into strips and lay them around your mount. Hold them in place with masking tape and then insert a pin centrally at each corner when you are happy with the position.

Carefully remove the strips and, very lightly, mark guide lines for stencilling the border using a pencil and set-square. Check the lines are exactly the right distance from the oval shape and parallel to the outer edge. The stencils at the top and sides should be equidistant from the oval and the lower stencil slightly further away to look visually correct.

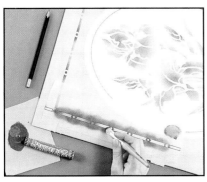

Finally, stencil the border in a single colour using stencil crayons as before. Build up the colour where the strips meet the round spots in the design to add interest. Assemble the stencil with the mount and a piece of glass in a simple frame coloured to complement your flowers and decorations.

Suggested size: One square represents 2.5cm (1in).

Hang this Oriental mobile at a window and watch the sun shine through the coloured tissue paper. Use the template on page 25 to cut out a pair of lanterns in black cardboard. Cut out all the sections, taking care not to cut through any of the 'bridges'.

To achieve the stained glass effect, cut out coloured tissue paper a little larger than the sections to be covered. Glue the pieces of tissue paper to the back of one lantern. Trim the edges. Glue a silky red tassel to hang from the bottom of one lantern. Now glue the two lanterns together enclosing the tissue paper. Suspend the mobile on red embroidery thread.

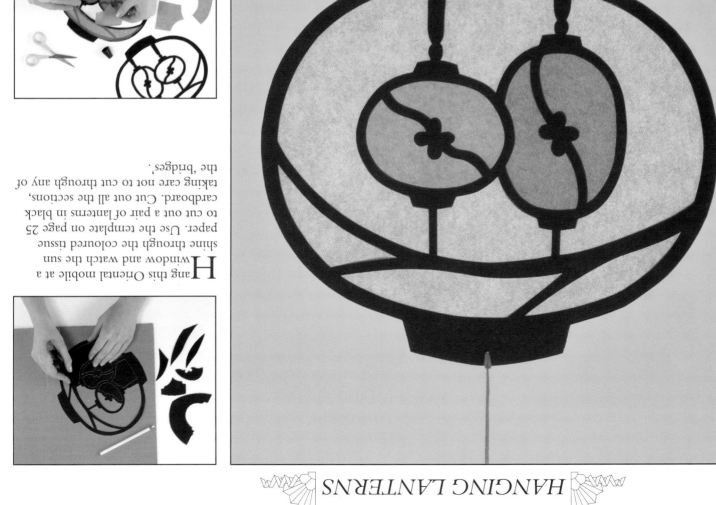

Here are templates and diagrams for several of the projects in the preceeding chapter. These need to be enlarged as follows: draw a grid of 3cm (1¼in) squares, then copy the design onto your grid, square by square, using the lines as a guide.

The clock is constructed from measurements. Use a ruler and set square to draw the shape onto cardboard and follow either the metric or imperial measurements but not a combination of the two.

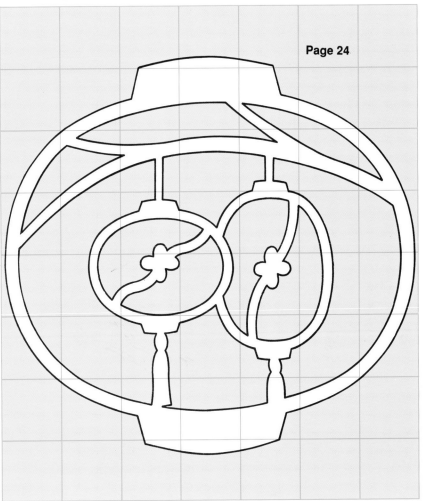

Page 24

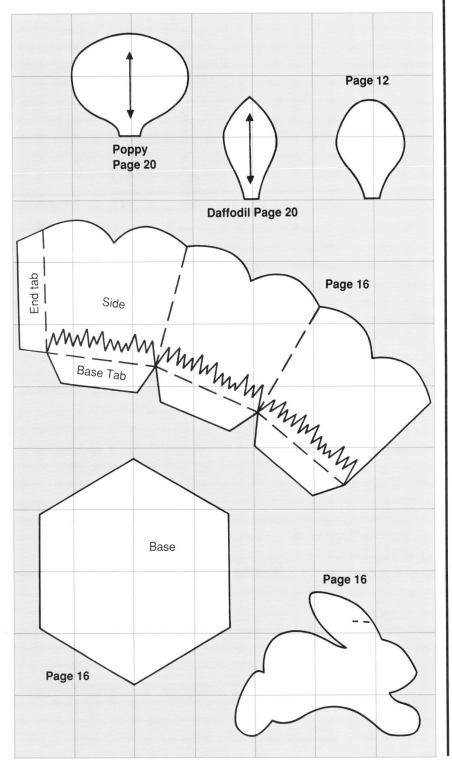

Page 12

Poppy
Page 20

Daffodil Page 20

Page 16

End tab

Side

Base Tab

Base

Page 16

Page 16

Page 18

20cm (8¼in)   3.5cm (1⅜in)   3.5cm (1⅜in)   20cm (8¼in)   3.5cm (1⅜in)   3.5cm (1⅜in)

Back

Front

4cm (1⅝in)

5cm (2in)

Base

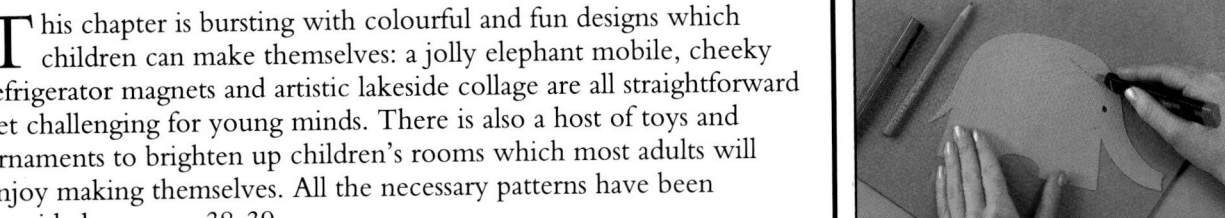

DESIGNS FOR CHILDREN

This chapter is bursting with colourful and fun designs which children can make themselves: a jolly elephant mobile, cheeky refrigerator magnets and artistic lakeside collage are all straightforward yet challenging for young minds. There is also a host of toys and ornaments to brighten up children's rooms which most adults will enjoy making themselves. All the necessary patterns have been provided on pages 38-39.

Do ensure that children are supervised if cutting out is involved. Most paper items can be successfully cut using children's safety scissors, but tougher cardboard may need to be cut by an adult with a craft knife.

Here is a mobile for animal lovers – a small herd of elephants. Cut out four elephants in co-ordinating coloured cardboard using the template on page 38. Draw eyes on both sides with a felt-tipped pen and cut slits along the broken lines with a craft knife. Make a hole with a thick needle at the top of the elephant.

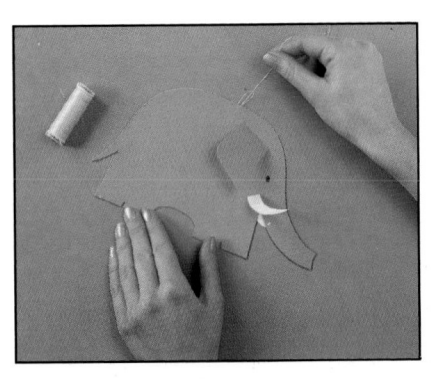

Make a pattern of the ear and tusk. Fold coloured cardboard in half and place the ear pattern on top, matching the broken line to the fold. Draw around the ear and cut it out. Cut out the tusks in white cardboard in the same way. Insert the ears and tusks halfway through the slits and bend them downwards.

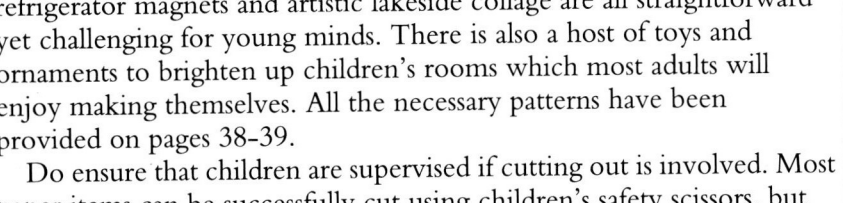

Cut four 45cm (18in) lengths of thread. Loop the threads in half and insert the ends through the hole. Pull the ends through the loop so the elephant hangs from the thread. Knot the ends together and hang on mobile wires. You could spray paint the wires to match the elephants. Hang the mobile on a length of thread.

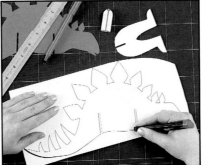

Now you can have your very own prehistoric monster – a Stegosaurus dinosaur. Refer to the template on page 38 to make a pattern of the dinosaur body and two sets of legs on thin cardboard. Draw around the patterns onto mounting board (use a board that is six sheets thick). Cut out the sections with a craft knife.

Slot the legs and body together, placing the smaller set of legs at the front, as shown.

What better way to invite friends to a party at the local hop than with this funny frog. Draw a frog with large, bulging eyes on thin green cardboard and cut it out. Cut out a narrow smiling mouth.

Glue on a pair of joggle eyes and write a message on the back. Now all you need is the party . . .

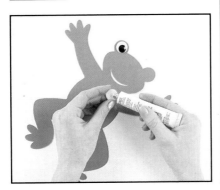

These funny glasses are sure to amuse all who see them. Cut a pattern using the template on page 39 and use to cut a blue cardboard front. Cut out the windows and use as a guide to cut two lenses from green transparent acetate, adding 1cm (³⁄₈in) to the edges all round. Glue the lenses behind the windows.

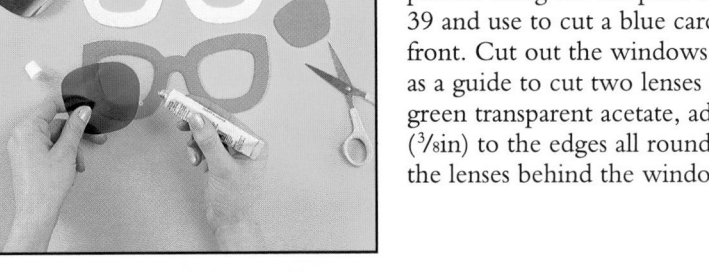

Use the template to cut out a pair of palm trees – cut the trunks in brown cardboard and leaves in green cardboard. Glue the palm trees each side of the front piece.

Cut out a pair of arms in blue cardboard using the template. Score the ends along the broken lines and bend back the tabs at right angles. Glue the tabs behind the glasses to complete.

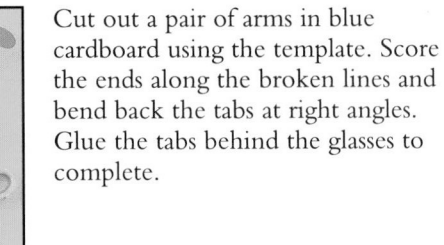

Textured papers make an interesting collage. Cut pale blue cardboard 30cm x 24cm (12in x 9¹⁄₂in) for the background. Cover the lower 11cm (4¹⁄₄in) with clear sticky-backed plastic. Cut a strip of pale green cardboard and tear away one long edge. Glue the strip above the 'lake'. Cut pointed strips of green gummed paper and stick over the join.

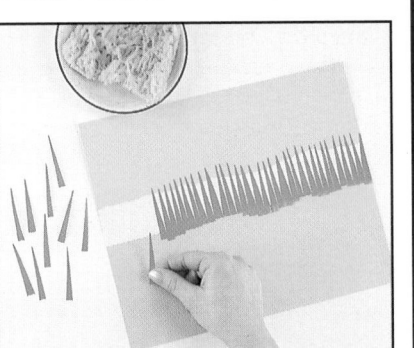

Use the template on page 39 to cut out the swan and wing in wavy textured paper. Cut the beak in orange paper and glue behind the swan. Draw the swan's eye with a black felt-tipped pen. Glue the swan to the middle of the lake and glue the wing on top.

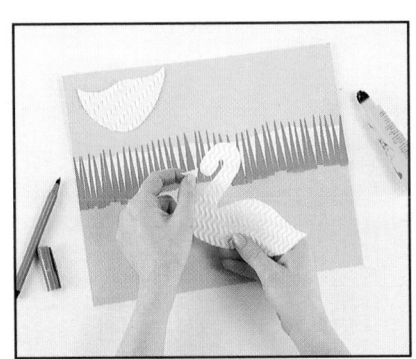

Cut very thin strips of brown cardboard for the bullrush stems and three long leaves from green crepe paper. Glue the leaves and stems to the picture. Cut bullrushes from black flock sticky-backed plastic and glue over the top of the stems. Use the template to cut out three lily pads in green cardboard and glue to the lake.

Cast a spooky glow at a Halloween gathering with this eerie lantern. Cut a strip 50cm x 22cm (20in x 8½in) of shiny black cardboard – the sort that is white on the other side. Cut out a large and a small bat from thin cardboard and use as templates to draw three bats on the back of the strip.

When you have finished tracing the bats, carefully cut them out using a craft knife.

This jolly hippo will brighten the kitchen when stuck to the fridge door with a small magnet. Roughly cut out a design from some left-over wrapping paper. Stick the motif to a piece of thick cardboard with spray glue.

Overlap the ends of the strip and staple them together. To complete the effect, place a few nightlights inside the lantern. Do not leave the lantern unattended when it is lit.

Cut out the picture with a craft knife. Do not attempt to cut right through the board in one go, but gradually cut deeper and deeper until you reach the cutting board.

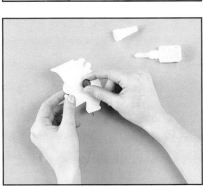

Glue a fridge magnet to the back of the character. Magnets are available at many art and craft shops.

This is a traditional kite with a difference – there is an amusing clown's face on the front. To make the frame you will need two lengths of wood dowel; one 84cm (33in) long and the other 56cm (22in). Cut two small notches 5mm (¼in) from the ends of both sticks with a craft knife.

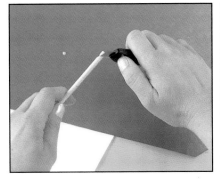

Mark the short stick at the centre and the long stick 28cm (11in) from one end. Lay the sticks across one another at right angles matching the marks, and bind tightly with fine string. Secure with a dab of glue. Tie string around the notches at one end of a stick, then wind it tightly around the other notches as shown and knot the ends of string together.

Butt the edges of a white and a green piece of paper together with the wrong sides uppermost. Lay the kite frame on top and cut around it 1.5cm (⅝in) outside the string. Cut off the corners level with the notches. Remove the frame and join the butted edges together with masking tape.

The method for making this traditional pinwheel is Origami, which is the ancient Japanese craft of paper folding. Start with a 20cm (8in) square of patterned paper. Fold the side edges to meet at the centre then fold the top and bottom edges to meet at the centre as well.

Apply double-sided tape to the edges of the kite covering on the wrong side. Place the frame on top and fold over the edges enclosing the string.

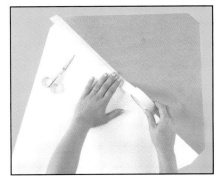

Now bring the side corners at the centre to the top and bottom edges with a diagonal fold.

Cut a 112cm (44in) length of string and tie the ends to the top and bottom notch. Cut a 92cm (36¼in) length and tie the ends to the side notches. Balance the kite by resting the strings on a finger and fastening them together with a curtain ring where they cross over. Decorate the front with ribbons and paper shapes. Finally, tie a ball of string to the ring.

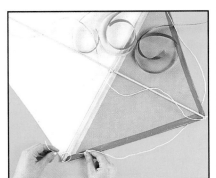

Open the diagonal folds out flat then lightly hold at the centre and pull each corner of the square underneath to the outside. Turn alternate points in opposite directions to form the pinwheel. Attach the pinwheel to a painted balsa wood stick with a drawing pin.

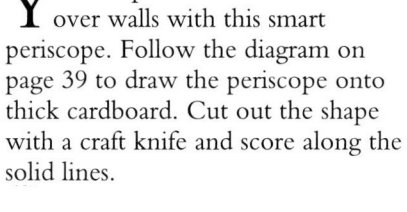

Y ou can peer around corners and over walls with this smart periscope. Follow the diagram on page 39 to draw the periscope onto thick cardboard. Cut out the shape with a craft knife and score along the solid lines.

Bend the periscope backwards along the scored lines so you can see how it will look when finished. Flatten out the periscope and glue a small make-up mirror on the wrong side in the middle of the base and top.

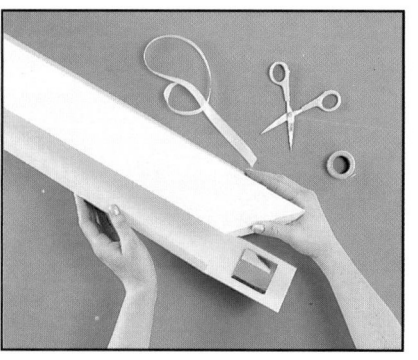

Bend the periscope back into shape and stick the long tab under the opposite long edge with double-sided tape.

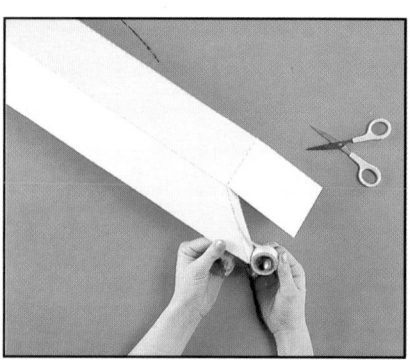

Stick the remaining tabs to the base and top with double-sided tape.

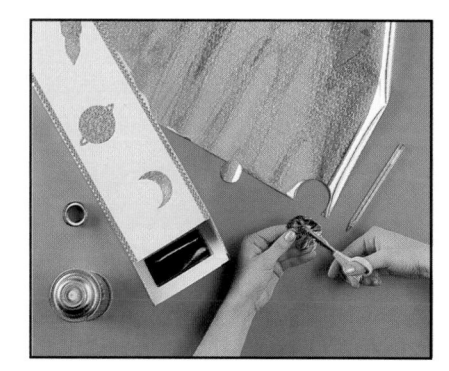

Apply decorative sticky tape over all the folds to neaten and reinforce the edges. Cut out space rockets and planets from giftwrap and stick to the periscope with spray glue.

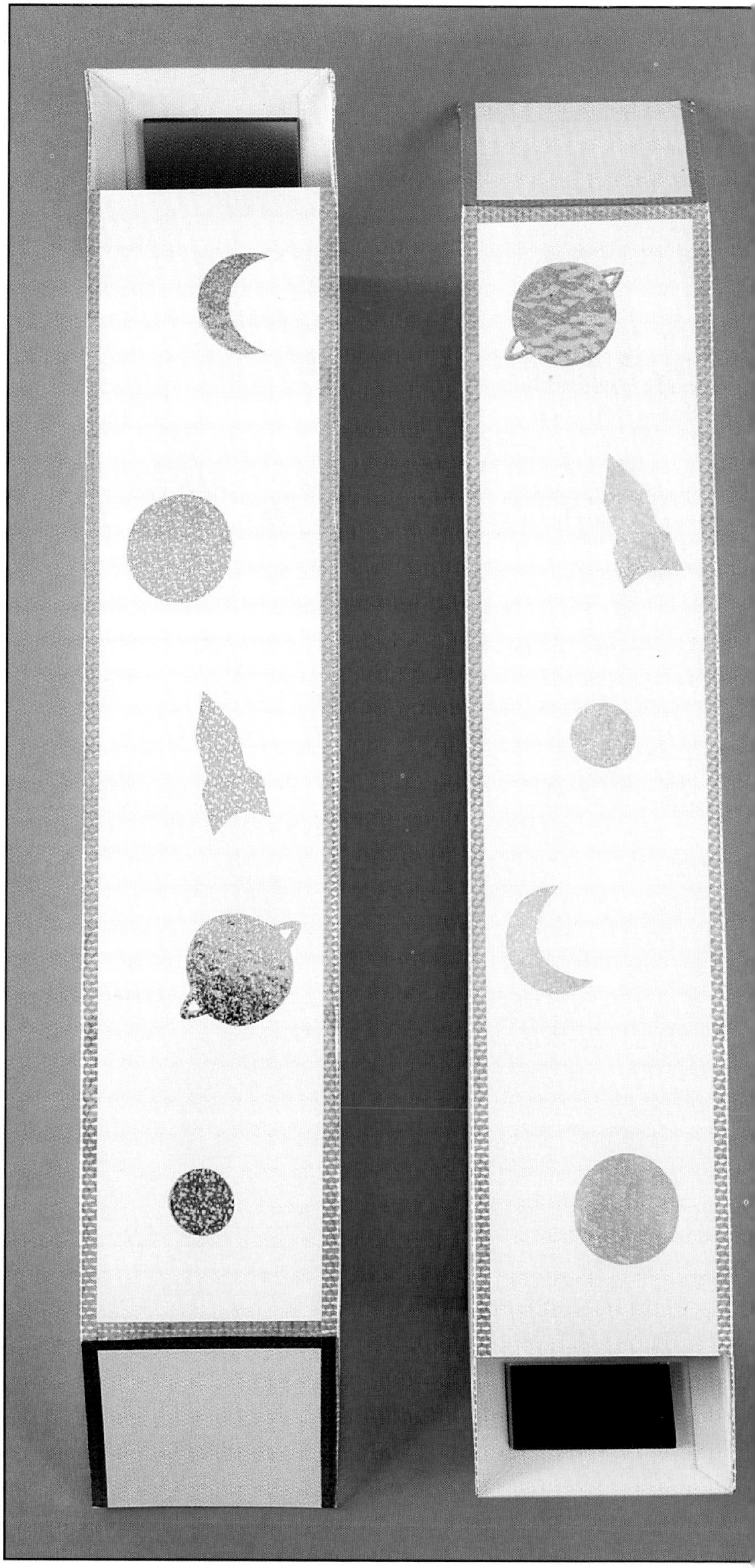

This clown is fun to make and not as difficult as he may seem. First cut a rectangle of crepe paper for the body 30cm x 24cm (12in x 9½in). Overlap the shorter edges and glue them together making a tube. Push toy filling inside and stuff the tube firmly. With a needle and thread, gather the open ends tightly, enclosing the filling.

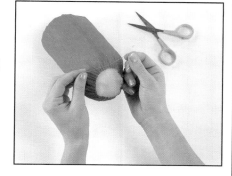

Cut two 14cm (5½in) squares of crepe paper for the sleeves and make two tubes like the body. For the arms, cut two pink pipecleaners 16cm (6¼in) long. Insert each arm into a sleeve and glue across one end, sandwiching the arm in the middle. Gently push toy filling inside around the arm.

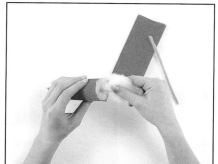

Bend over the end of the arms in a hook to imitate hands. Gather the sleeves tightly above the hands with a needle and thread, making a frilled edge. Glue the flat ends of the sleeves to the body.

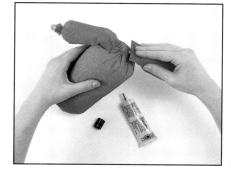

Cut a strip of crepe paper 35cm x 6cm (14in x 2¼in), cutting the short ends parallel with the grain of the crepe paper. This will be the neck ruffle. Glue the ends together and gather one long edge. Pull up the gathers tightly like a rosette and glue the ruffle on top of the body.

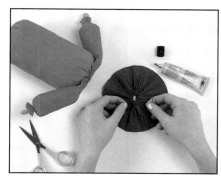

Take a 7cm (2¾in) diameter cotton pulp ball and glue a red bead in the middle for a nose. Draw eyes and a mouth with felt-tipped pens. Glue curly gift wrapping ribbon each side of the face. The hat is a 14cm (5½in) diameter circle of coloured cardboard. Cut to the centre and overlap the edges making a cone. Glue the edges together and glue the hat in place.

Glue the head on top of the ruffle. Using the template on page 39, cut out the shoes in coloured cardboard. Glue the body on top of the shoes and then glue some bright pom-poms to the hat, shoes and front of the body. This clown is not for playing with but is a charming ornament for a child's room.

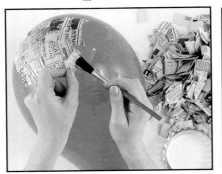

This lion mask is made from papier-mâché moulded over a balloon. Blow up the balloon and tie a knot in the end. Tear newspaper into small pieces and then dilute PVA medium with water to thin it slightly. Spread a little of the solution on the front of the balloon and cover with the newspaper pieces.

Cover one half of the balloon with about seven layers of papier-mâché and leave to dry overnight. Gently pull the balloon away from the mask and trim the edges of the mask with a pair of scissors. Cut out two round holes for the eyes. Paint the mask with non-toxic ochre coloured paint and then paint a black nose and muzzle, as shown.

To make the mane, cut brown crepe paper 140cm x 16cm (55in x 6¼in) and fold lengthwise in half. Cut a fringe along the long edges. With a needle and long length of thread, gather up the mane close to the fold. Glue the mane around the lion's face. Finally, staple a length of thin elastic to each side of the back of the mask, to fit.

Make this colourful head-dress and join the tribe! Cut a 4cm (1½in) wide strip of red cardboard 60cm (24in) long. Cut out simple shapes from coloured papers and glue to the strip.

Although a bit more complicated to make than a cardboard mask, this mask will last much longer. The face is made from papier-mâché (see page 34 for instructions); the mould is a balloon. Blow the balloon up as big as you can without bursting it, and build up the papier-mâché over at least one half. When it is dry, gently let the air out of the balloon by piercing the knotted end.

Trim the mask down, cutting the pointed end into a forehead. Cut out circular eyes and a curved mouth. Now give the mould a coat of white emulsion (water-based paint), sand it down and give it another two coats to make it as smooth a surface as possible.

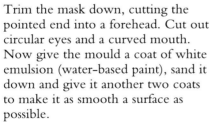

Overlap the ends of the strip and glue together. Stick three coloured quill feathers upright behind the strip with sticky tape.

Cut six 2.5cm (1in) wide strips of black crepe paper 40cm (16in) long. Spread paper glue along one long edge and fold the strips in half. Staple three lengths together at one end and make a plait. Bind the end with embroidery thread and make another plait in the same way. Stick the plaits to each side of the head-dress with sticky tape.

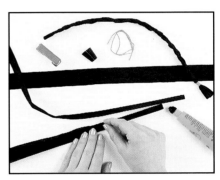

Around each eye paint four slightly triangular stripes. Also paint large red lips and cheeks on either side. For the nose, paint a ping pong ball red and glue it in place. For the hair, cut short lengths of yarn and attach them to strips of sticky tape; stick these to the back of the mask. Finally, take a piece of elastic, staple it to either side, and paint over the staples with a touch more emulsion.

Create this unusual birthday table decoration, using the template on page 39 to cut a base and lid in white cardboard. Cut the end tab off the lid. Now cut a strip of mottled brown cardboard 30cm x 6cm (12in x 2¼in). Tear a thin strip of shiny red paper and glue along the middle of the 'sponge'. Score across the strip at the centre and 1.5cm (⅝in) from the ends.

Score the base and lid along the broken lines and snip the end tab to the scored line. Bend all the pieces backwards along the scored lines. Glue the 'sponge' to the side tabs on the base with the folds at the corners. Cut pale blue cardboard 12cm x 6cm (4¾in x 2¼in) and glue one long edge over the end tabs.

Cut two 12cm (4¾in) long strips of white cardboard and cut scallops along one edge. Glue to the blue end as icing. Glue one tab of the lid inside the top of the box. Cut a strip of blue cardboard for the candle. Make a 'flame' from a foil sweet (candy) wrapper and glue to one end. Fold under the other end of the candle and glue to the lid.

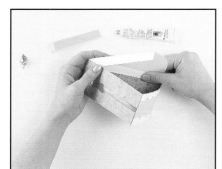

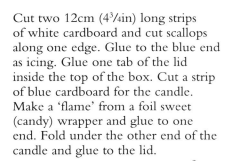

Glass paperweights such as these (available in kit form from craft shops) are ideal for making novel presents. Kids in particular will enjoy making this design. To work out a mosaic picture, draw a grid of squares about 4mm (³⁄₁₆in) apart. Trace around the paperweight template onto the grid and draw a design. Colour the picture as a guide for the finished mosaic.

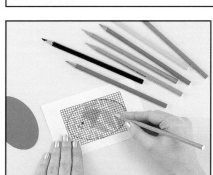

Cut out tiny squares of coloured paper the same size as the grid squares. Draw a cross on a piece of paper to help keep the mosaic squares straight. Spread paper glue thinly along part of one line and press the squares in place. Nudge them into position with scissors or tweezers. Follow the grid design and glue on all the squares.

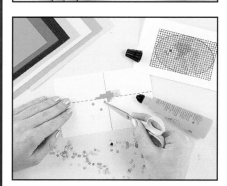

Use the paperweight template to cut the mosaic to fit the paperweight. Turn the paperweight upside down and lay the mosaic in the hollow. Peel the paper off the sticky-backed flock backing and carefully stick it over the back of the paperweight enclosing the mosaic.

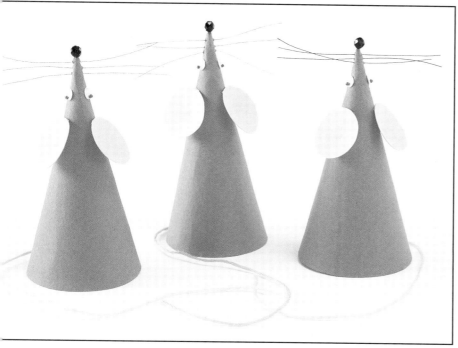

These amusing finger puppets are sure to entertain your friends. Use the template on page 39 to cut out the dancer in pale pink cardboard. Cut out the dress in shiny, deep pink cardboard and glue to the puppet. Next cut an 8cm (3in) diameter circle from the centre of a white paper doily for a petticoat and glue to the dress with spray glue.

Colour the hair, draw the eyes and lightly mark the nose with a black felt-tipped pen. Draw the mouth with a red felt-tipped pen and rouge the cheeks with a red coloured pencil.

Play to the gallery with this finger puppet trio of tiny friends. Cut out a quarter-circle of thin magenta cardboard with a 9cm (3½in) radius. Pull between thumb and finger to curve the piece. Overlap the straight edges to form a cone and glue the edges together.

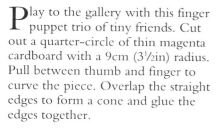

Mark the finger hole positions on the petticoat and carefully cut through all the layers with a craft knife.

Glue a small black bead to the point of the cone as a nose and then glue two small joggle eyes each side. To make the ears, cut out two small circles of thin pink cardboard. Cut to the centre and overlap the cut edges. Glue the overlapped edges together then glue the ears to the cone.

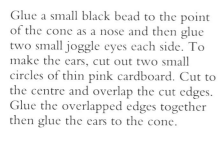

Take some toy-making whiskers and thread on a needle through the top of the cone. Drop a little glue onto the whiskers inside the cone to secure them. Trim the ends level. Thread a length of embroidery thread on a needle and attach to the base of the mouse at the back as a tail. Knot the thread inside the finger puppet.

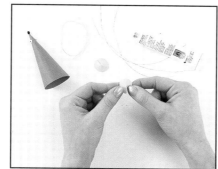

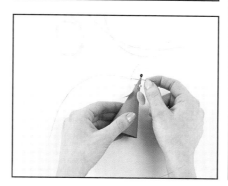

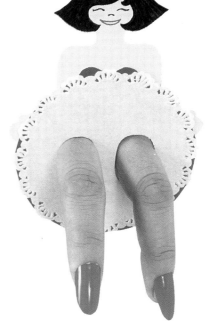

Size up patterns as described on page 25, making each square of your grid measure 3cm (1¼in).

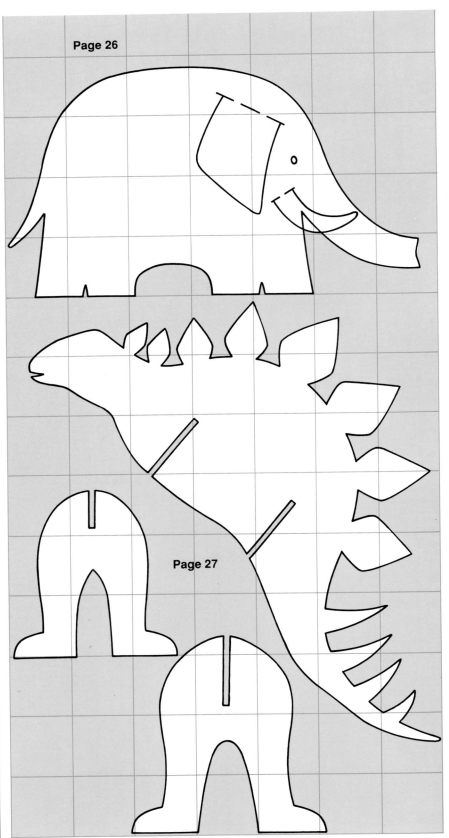

Page 26

Page 27

Papier-mâché is very durable and can be made in many ways. This traditional method uses a paste of flour and water. Tear up wallpaper lining paper into small pieces. Then grease the inside of a small bowl with Vaseline. Brush the paper pieces with paste and stick them inside the bowl, starting at the centre and working outwards.

Build up three layers of papier-mâché and leave to dry overnight. Apply at least four more layers. When the papier-mâché is completely dry, remove it from the bowl mould. Trim the top edge level with a pair of scissors. Paint the bowl with a craft paint, sanding between coats. Cut coloured tissue paper into small triangles.

Stick the triangles to the bowl with a clear varnish such as PVA medium. Once the bowl is decorated, coat it inside and out with the varnish. Line the bowl with tissue paper and fill it with pretty bathroom accessories.

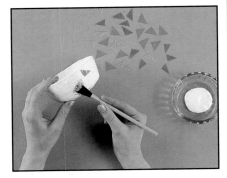

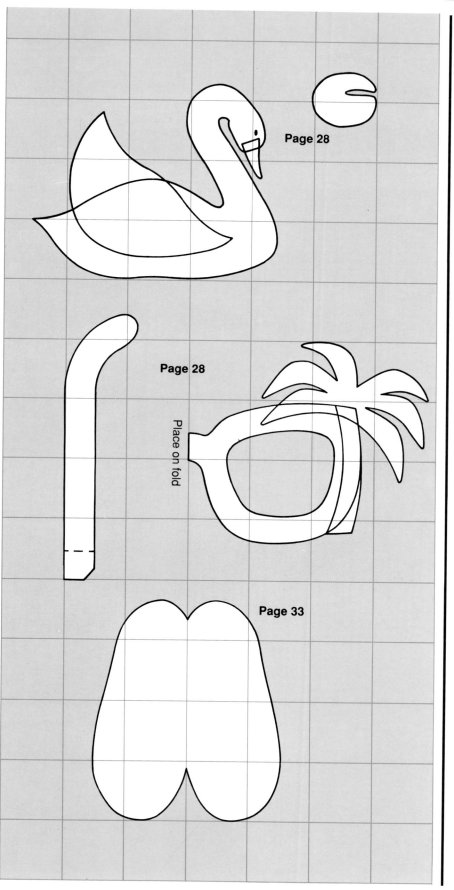

Page 28

Page 28

Place on fold

Page 33

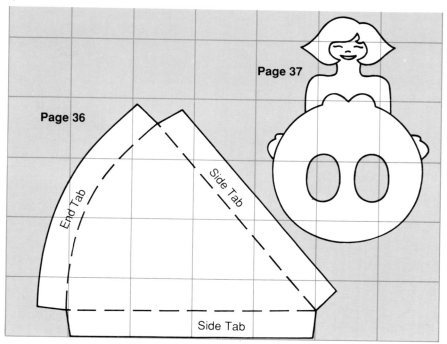

Page 37

Page 36

End Tab

Side Tab

Side Tab

Page 32

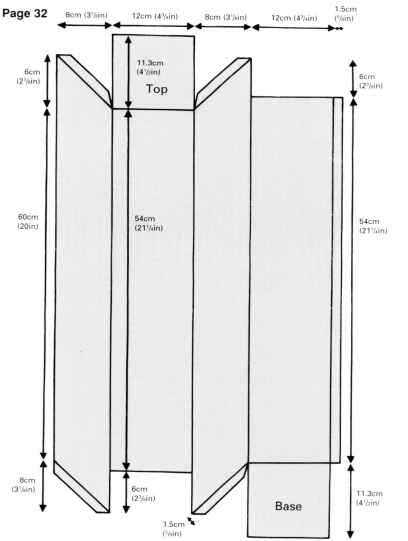

8cm (3¹⁄₈in) 12cm (4³⁄₄in) 8cm (3¹⁄₈in) 12cm (4³⁄₄in) 1.5cm (⁵⁄₈in)

11.3cm (4¹⁄₂in)

Top

6cm (2³⁄₈in)

6cm (2³⁄₈in)

60cm (20in)

54cm (21¹⁄₄in)

54cm (21¹⁄₄in)

8cm (3¹⁄₈in)

6cm (2³⁄₈in)

Base

11.3cm (4¹⁄₂in)

1.5cm (⁵⁄₈in)

Don't spend a fortune buying party decorations, as this chapter will show you how to create a wide range of stunning effects at a low cost. From graceful paper garlands, to stylish fancy hats and jewelled masks, Christmas ornaments and festive wreaths, we include all that you might need to make your home look as festive as possible, and get everyone in the party mood. There are also designs to create your very own Advent Calendar, a pretty garland on which to hang your Christmas cards and a super winter sleigh to fill with sweets for a table centrepiece. Where possible we have included templates on page 59 to assist you.

Pull the cord and watch Santa dance. Use the template on page 59 to cut out the cardboard pieces. Cut one body and a pair of arms and legs from red cardboard. Mark the crosses on the back. Cut a pink face and glue to the head. Cut a white hat brim and beard, bobble and two cuffs. Glue the hat brim and beard over the face and the bobble to the top of the hat.

Cut out two green mittens, a black belt and two boots. Butt the straight ends of the mittens and arms together and glue cuffs over the joins. Wrap gold sticky tape around the middle of the belt and glue to the body. Glue the boot tops under the legs. Cut out a pink nose and glue on the face. Draw the eyes and mouth with felt-tipped pens.

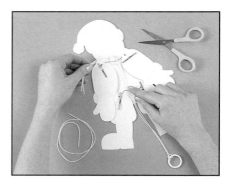

Mark dots on the limbs and attach to the body with paper fasteners at the crosses. Pull the limbs downwards on the back and tie the arms together with thread fastened through the dots. Tie the legs in the same way. Thread a small ring onto a double length of fine cord. Knot the cord around the legs' thread and then the arms' thread.

Cut a 3cm (1¼in) square of cardboard to use as a template for the doors. Draw around the square twenty-three times on the back of the tree, positioning the doors at random but leaving the trunk clear. Cut three sides of the doors, leave the right hand side 'hinged' so the door opens the right way on the other side.

On the right side of the tree, score the hinged side of each door lightly so it will open easily – but do not open the doors yet. Number the doors one to twenty-three with a silver pen.

Cut out small Christmas pictures from wrapping paper and used greeting cards. On the back of the tree, stick each picture behind a door by spreading paper glue on the tree around the doors.

Decorate the calendar with a gold star on the top and circles of metallic cardboard between the doors.

This Advent calendar can be used every year at Christmas. First make the Christmas tree pattern. Cut a piece of paper measuring about 63cm x 50cm (25in x 20in) and fold in half lengthwise. Draw half the tree with a trunk against the foldline and cut it out. Open out flat and use the pattern as a template to cut out the tree in green cardboard.

Write the number twenty-four on the front of a small red gift box with a silver pen. Stick a ribbon rosette on the top and glue the box onto the tree trunk. Fill the box with sweets. To finish, stick a picture hanger on the back of the calendar at the top.

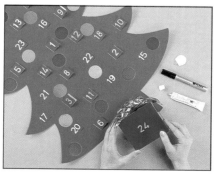

These miniature lanterns make attractive Christmas tree ornaments. First take a piece of foil-covered paper 11cm (5½in) square. Fold it in half, and rule a line 1.5cm (¾in) from the loose edges. Now rule lines 1cm (½in) apart, from the fold up to this first line. Cut along these lines and open out the sheet of paper.

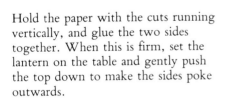

Hold the paper with the cuts running vertically, and glue the two sides together. When this is firm, set the lantern on the table and gently push the top down to make the sides poke outwards.

Finally, cut a strip of matching paper 13cm (5in) long and 1cm (½in) wide. Dab some glue on each end, and glue the strip onto the inside of the lantern, at the top, for a handle.

If you haven't any shiny bells for the Christmas tree, it's not difficult to make some from foil, beads and a little string. First take a saucer and mark around it onto the back of some coloured foil. Cut out the circle, then fold it in half, and cut along the fold line. Fold each half of the circle into a cone and glue it in place.

For the clapper, string a bead onto a length of thread — preferably waxed — and tie a knot over the bead. Lay the thread against the bell so that the clapper is at the right level, then tie a knot level with the hole in the top. This prevents the string from being pulled through the hole when threaded. Pull the string through the hole from the inside and thread on a smaller bead at the top; knot in place.

Finish each bell by dabbing a little glue around the bottom edge and sprinkling on some glitter. When you have made three bells, string them together, and attach them to a ring so that they can be hung on the tree. Wind a little tinsel wire around the string, and tie a couple of bows for that final touch of glamour.

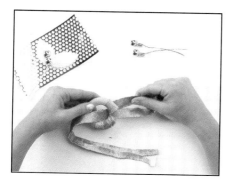

Add a touch of regal splendour to your tree with these golden decorations. To make a miniatrue wreath, first wind the wires of two silk leaves and two small glass balls together, and bind with white florists' tape. Cut a 16cm (6½in) length from sequin waste. Next cut a long strip of gold crepe paper, fold the edges in and bind around a small wooden ring.

Tie a loop of gold thread around the ring at the paper join. Twist the leaf and ball stems around the ring over the thread, folding in the wire ends to secure.

Fold the ends of the sequin waste into the centre so that they overlap, with the selvedges at each side. Thread a long length of fine florists' wire down the middle, through all the layers. Then thread the wire back and pull up gently to make a bow shape. Twist the wires tightly to secure and bind them around the leaf wires. Arrange the leaves, bow and balls attractively over the ring.

To make a jewelled sphere, first wrap a polystyrene ball with gold crepe paper: cut a square of paper to fit generously, and pull it up tightly over the ball. Tie firmly around the gathered paper with a length of gold thread, and knot the ends of the thread to make a hanging loop. Cut a strip of crepe paper to make a bow and fold the raw edges in. Pinch the strip into a bow shape.

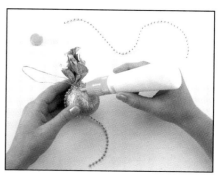

Run a line of clear adhesive around the ball and press a strip of beading trim into it. Repeat with a line of beading crossing in the opposite direction. Stick 'jewels' between the beads and large sequins, held in place with a pearl-headed pin. Trim the paper at the top of the sphere and attach the bow with a sequin trimmed pearl-headed pin.

From cartridge paper cut two rectangles, one 58cm x 10cm (23in x 4in), the other 58cm x 6.5cm (23in x 2½in). Mark each one into 12mm (½in) strips and draw a line 2.5cm (1in) from the long edge. Following your marks, cut out a zig-zag edge and pleat the strips. Use spray adhesive to stick gold foil to each side of the large rectangle, and silver foil to the smaller one.

Pleat the gold strip again and fold it into a circle. Join the two ends with double-sided tape or glue and prevent the centre from popping up by smearing glue into the centre. Weight down the star with a book until it is dry. Next make a loop from gold thread from which to hang the star, and glue this to the centre of the star at the back.

Make these delightful baskets to hang on your tree. Measure 4cm (1½in) up from the base of a yoghourt carton and cut round. Cut a 20cm (8in) diameter circle from crepe paper and cover the pot, stretching the paper up over the edges. Cover a cardboard circle with crepe paper to fit inside the base. Cut a handle 22cm (8½in) x 1.5cm (½in) from thin cardboard and cover.

Make up the silver star as before and place a double-sided adhesive pad on the centre back. Use this to attach the star to the gold star, aligning the pleats. Finally, put a little glue into the centre of the star and press a small glass ball in place.

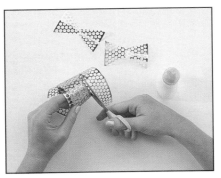

From sequin foil waste cut a strip long enough to wrap around the pot. Run a line of glue along the top and bottom of the pot and in one vertical line. Wrap the foil round, pressing into the glue, and trim, straightening the overlap along the vertical line of glue. Cut two strips 5cm (2in) wide from sequin waste, fold in half, selvedges level, and cut into bow shapes.

Staple the handle and foil bows each side of the basket. Tie bows from lengths of satin ribbon and stick over the foil bows with double-sided tape. Stick a double-sided adhesive pad in the bottom of the basket and arrange a bunch of glass balls on top.

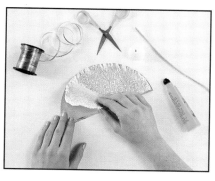

Cut a 10cm (4in) diameter semi-circle of silver cardboard, silver crepe paper and crinkly film. Trim the curve of the film in zig-zags and flute the crepe paper curve between your thumb and finger. Place the crepe paper on the cardboard with the film on top and glue together along the straight edges. Overlap the straight edges in a cone and glue.

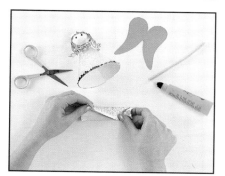

Draw eyes with a black pen on a 3.5cm (1½in) diameter cotton pulp ball. Cut short pieces of narrow giftwrap ribbon and glue to the head as a fringe. Cut longer pieces and pull the ends over a knife blade to curl them, then glue over the head. Glue ribbon around the head, then cut a slit in the base of the head and push the cone point through.

Cut silver crepe paper 11cm x 6cm (4½in x 2¼in) and flute the ends. Glue the long edges together and insert a 15cm (6in) pipecleaner for the arms through the tube and bend back the ends. Squeeze the centre and glue behind the cone, bending the arms forward. Use the template on page 59 to cut silver cardboard wings and glue them in place behind the angel.

To make these pretty silver bells cut out two bell shapes from cardboard. Peel the backing off some silver sticky-backed plastic and place the cut-outs on top, pressing firmly; then cut around them.

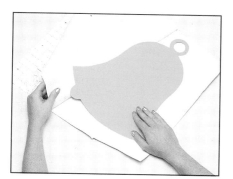

Glue the loops at the top of the bells together, spreading the bell shapes apart as shown.

Curl some gift wrap ribbon by running the blunt edge of a scissors blade along it; attach the ribbon to the bells. Finish off with a bow tied through the loops and some tiny birds cut from foil paper. The template for these is superimposed on the bell template.

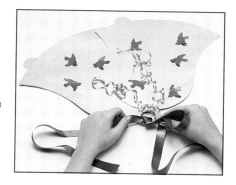

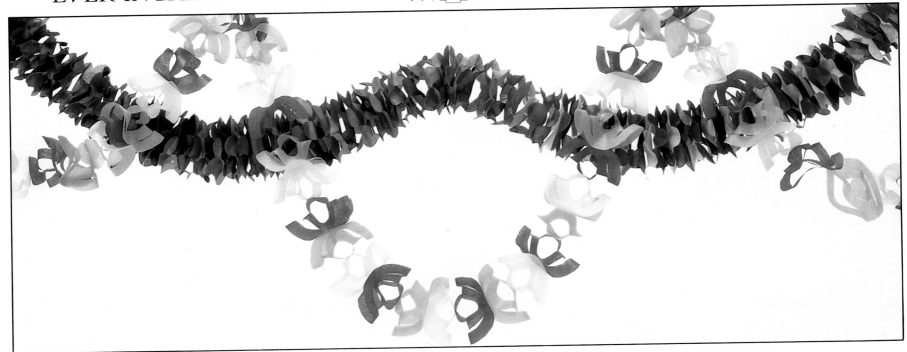

This graceful paper chain is made from circular pieces of tissue paper. First cut two circles of cardboard and lots of circles of tissue paper, all 10cm (4in) in diameter. Take about ten tissue paper circles and fold them together in four. If you use more than about ten layers, the folds won't be as good.

Now make two curved cuts as shown, from the single-folded edge almost to the double folds. Open out the circles. Glue the centre of the first circle to the middle of one cardboard circle.

Next, take the second tissue circle and glue it to the first at the top and bottom. Glue the third circle to the centre of the second circle. Continue in this way remembering to glue alternate circles in the same place at the top and bottom. If you alter the positioning you will spoil the effect. Finally glue the other cardboard circle to the last tissue circle to complete the garland.

Another simple garland made from tissue paper. Cut out a cardboard pattern from the template on page 59. Now cut out lots of flower shapes from tissue paper, using several different colours.

To start the garland, dab a little glue (one that won't soak through the thin paper) onto alternate petals of the first flower. Place the second flower on top and press them together.

Now on the second flower dab glue on the petals lying between those glued on the first flower. Take the third flower and press it firmly on top. Continue in this way, gluing petals in alternate positions, until the garland is long enough. Cut two extra cardboard shapes from the pattern and glue them to either end. Onto these tape a little loop of cord for hanging the garland.

This garland is made from different coloured tissue paper stars. Refer to the template on page 59 to make the basic pattern from thin paper. Fold up to six layers of tissue paper into quarters, place a quarter of the paper pattern on top, edges level, and cut out. Fold the tissue paper in half again, (separate some of the layers if too bulky) and cut two slits in the positions marked in the photograph below. Cut a collection of different coloured tissue paper 'stars' in this way, plus two stars cut from cartridge paper for the garland ends. Glue a tissue star to each paper star using spray adhesive. Stick a small piece of double-sided tape to the centre of one tissue star and press this onto the centre of the tissue-covered paper star.

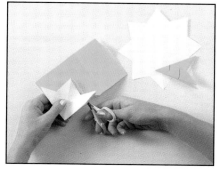

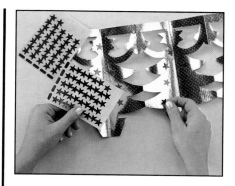

Next, place double-sided tape on four opposite points of the tissue star, and stick another star on top, aligning the points and slits. Keep repeating the sequence, pressing pieces of double-sided tape alternately to the centre, then to the four points, of each star, building up the layers until the garland is the required length. Finish by attaching the other end section.

U se this attractive frieze to decorate shelves, or to hang along a wall. From a length of foil gift wrap cut a long strip 23cm (9in) wide. Make a tree template from paper using the pattern on page 59 and line it up along one short edge of the gift wrap. Draw around the outline marking a fold line down the centre of the tree shape. Mark an X on each section to be cut out.

Fold the gift wrap concertina fashion along its length and staple the layers together above and below the pattern area to prevent the folds from slipping. Cut out through all the layers, using a craft knife to cut out the enclosed areas between the star and the bell shapes. Be careful not to cut through the folds at the edge.

Open the frieze out. The foil can be left in gentle folds, or pressed flat with a cool iron. Stick self-adhesive foil stars all over the trees. You can make the frieze to the required length simply by joining several frieze strips together, end to end, with sticky tape.

To make this festive ring, cut a long strip of crepe paper from the length of the roll, and bind a 20cm (8in) embroidery ring, securing the ends with double-sided tape near the hanging loop. Cut narrow gold ribbon about 110cm (43in) long and wind around the ring, securing with tape. Cut the same length from a gold sequin strip and wind between the ribbon.

Cut a strip of red crepe paper 1m (40in) long and 20cm (8in) wide; fold in half lengthways. Cut the same length from sequin waste and place over the crepe strip. Bind the centre with a long piece of florists' wire and trim ends into V-shape. Measure 23cm (9in) each side of the centre, bind with wire and fold the strip into a bow shape, holding it in shape with an adhesive pad.

Use the trailing centre wires to secure the bow in position at the top of the ring and arrange the ribbon ends over the ring. Finally, wire three small glass balls together and wrap these around the bow centre.

HOLLY WREATH

H ang this everlasting wreath on the door for a warm welcome to your visitors. Cut 5cm (2in) squares of green crepe paper and stick a small piece of masking tape in the centre for extra strength. Cut the point off a cocktail stick and use to make holes in a polystyrene ring. Push each square into a hole with the blunt end of the stick.

Continue pushing in squares until the ring is hidden. Take some artificial red berries on wires and push them into the wreath at random to decorate.

Tie a large bow of red satin ribbon. Bend a length of wire into a 'U' shape and thread through the back of the bow. Push the ends of the wire into the wreath.

This is a fun and simple way to hang up your Christmas cards. Simply take three long pieces of gift wrap or woven ribbon in red, green and gold, and plait them tightly together. Knot them at each end to hold them in place.

Now take some clothes pegs, lay them on several sheets of newspaper and spray them with gold paint. Turn them until all the sides have been covered and leave them to dry.

Fasten the ribbon to the wall at each end, and use the gold pegs to attach your Christmas cards to it. (If you prefer, and if you have some to spare, you could use tinsel instead of ribbon.)

Here is a lovely sparkly garland to hang at Christmastime. If you want to make it for a birthday party instead, substitute little boxed gifts and bottles for the bells, and make trees in pastel colours. Cut the chosen shapes from foil-covered cardboard, marking them out on the wrong side. Be careful when cutting as foil cardboard tends to crinkle at the edges.

Make a tiny hole in the top of each, using a hole punch, or the tip of a skewer. Using red twine, tie each shape to a long strand of tinsel, leaving even spaces between them. At the top of each bell, fix a bow of gold-covered wire; on the trees, a little star.

F ill this sleigh with foil wrapped candies for a charming table centrepiece. Apply gold embossed paper to both sides of thick cardboard with spray glue and cut a pair of sleighs using the template on page 59. For the base, glue gold paper to both sides of a rectangle of thin cardboard 36cm x 16cm (14$\frac{1}{8}$in x 6$\frac{1}{4}$in).

Mark the broken lines on the sleighs. Score along the base 1.5cm ($\frac{5}{8}$in) from each long edge. Snip away tiny triangles up to the scored lines so that the base will bend easily. Bend the snipped edge backwards at right angles.

Glue the snipped edges between the sleighs along the broken lines and lower, straight edges. Use the template to cut out two flowers in red foil paper and two leaves in green. Glue two leaves under each flower and glue three sequins in the middle. Glue a flower to each side of the sleigh and line it with scrunched up iridescent film.

For a stunning party mask, buy a ready-moulded mask from a stationer's or toy shop. The half-mask shown here is coloured with oil stencil pencils. Start with the pink; apply a little to a piece of waxed paper, then pick it up on the stencil brush. Using a circular motion, cover about half the mask. Repeat with the blue, filling in the gaps and giving the eyes a semblance of eyeliner.

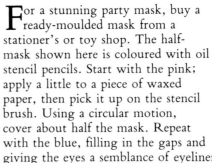

Next take a short length of lace and glue it to the back of the top half of the mask, down to where the elastic is attached. Glue some strands of curling gift wrap ribbon on either side. (Curl the ribbon by running the blunt edge of a pair of scissor along it.) Lastly, glue some large sequins over the tops of the ribbons to hide the ends, and glue another one in the centre of the forehead.

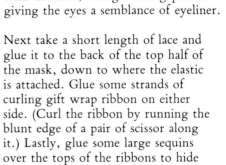

What could be simpler than these crisply-pleated paper fans, trimmed with curling ribbons? To begin, take a strip of printed wrapping paper and pleat it crosswise as shown.

For the black mask, first sew some silver tinsel wire around the edge and around the eyes. Sew on some pearl beads either side, then sew two or three grey or white feathers under the edges for an owlish look.

When you have finished the folding, hold the fan together by stapling it at one end. Cut some strips of gift wrap ribbon and run them along the edge of a ruler, or over a scissors blade, so that they curl.

Slip the ends of the ribbons between the folds of the fan and staple them in place. Finish by fixing a ribbon rosette over the stapled end.

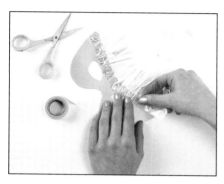

Another beautiful mask to make; this one is lavishly jewelled. Spray glue two pieces of gold cardboard together for extra strength, then use the template on page 59 to cut out the mask. Stick double-sided tape to the top edge on the back of the mask. Cut a strip of iridescent film 50cm x 6cm (20in x 2¼in). Scrunch up one long edge and press onto the tape.

Glue an iridescent plastic flower to the left-hand corner. Glue small glass stones at random to the mask and stick one in the centre of the flower. A pair of tweezers is useful for holding tiny stones. Glue gold plastic leaves around the flower.

Spray a 30cm (12in) length of thin wood dowel gold and bind with narrow giftwrap ribbon. Glue the ends in place. Pull two lengths of giftwrap ribbon between your thumb and finger to coil them. Stick the ribbons to one end of the dowel with sticky tape and use a strong glue to stick the wooden handle behind the mask.

Here's a jaunty majorette's cap that is ideal for a fancy dress party. Cut a strip of coloured cardboard 60cm x 13cm (24in x 5in). Use the template on page 59 to cut out a peak in silver cardboard. On the wrong side, score the peak along the broken lines and make snips in the cardboard to the scored line. Bend the snipped edge upwards.

Stick an 18cm (7 in) long strip of double-sided tape in the middle of one long edge of the hat on the wrong side. Overlap the ends of the strip and lightly hold together with masking tape. Press the snipped edge of the peak onto the sticky tape. Remove the masking tape.

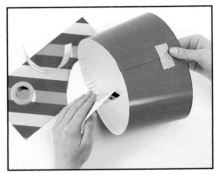

Wrap the hat around your head, overlapping the ends, and stick together with double-sided tape. Pleat a rectangle of foil giftwrap and bind the lower edge closed with clear sticky tape, forming a fan. Glue to the front of the hat. Finally, cut out a diamond shape from silver cardboard and glue it over the fan.

T hese conical hats are so easy to make that you will want to make one for each of your party guests. Cut a 30cm (12in) diameter circle of shiny cardboard for each hat and cut to the centre. Cut a slice out of the circle so that the hat is not too bulky. Overlap the cut edges and glue together.

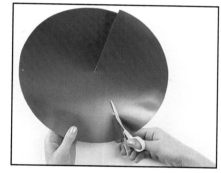

There are many ways to decorate the hats – stick on gold stars or use glitter pens to draw a pattern. Another idea is to spread glue in moon shapes on the hat and then sprinkle on glitter, shaking off the excess.

Make a hole with the points of a pair of scissors each side of the hat and thread with hat elastic. Adjust the elastic to fit under the chin and make a knot behind the holes.

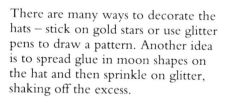

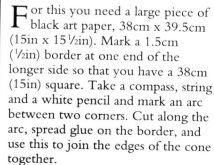

F or this you need a large piece of black art paper, 38cm x 39.5cm (15in x 15½in). Mark a 1.5cm (½in) border at one end of the longer side so that you have a 38cm (15in) square. Take a compass, string and a white pencil and mark an arc between two corners. Cut along the arc, spread glue on the border, and use this to join the edges of the cone together.

Use the cone to mark a circle on some black cardboard. Draw another line around the first, about 5cm (2in) from it, then another just 2.5cm (1in) inside the first line. Cut along the inner and outer lines, then make triangular cuts on the inside of the brim. Fold them up and glue them to the inside of the cone. Decorate the hat with gold stars and moons cut from sticky-backed plastic.

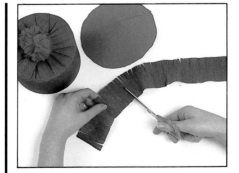

Essential wear at any children's party, these hats even bear the wearer's name. First cut the hats out of lightweight cardboard – a small circle and a rectangular piece for the fez and a semi-circular piece, about 15cm (6in) in diameter, for the conical hat. Glue the sides together to form a tube and a cone, and attach the top circle to the fez with tape. Cover the hats in crepe paper.

To make a tissue pom-pom, fold the tissue to get at least 12 layers, measuring 7cm (3in) square. Using a cup or glass, mark a circle on the paper, and cut it out. Staple the layers together at the centre. Cut strips into the centre, making them about 5mm (¼in) wide at the edge and stopping short of the staple. Fluff up the tissue paper to form a pom-pom.

Make pom-poms for both hats and attach them with glue or double-sided tape. Make a frill for the conical hat by cutting two lengths of crepe paper about 5cm (2in) deep and long enough to go around the edge of the rim. Neatly cut narrow strips about 2cm (¾in) deep on either side of the length to create a fringe. Staple the two layers of 'fringe' onto the rim of the hat.

Cut out paper letters from contrasting-coloured paper and glue names onto the front of each hat.

To make these fake neckties, first trace a pattern from a real necktie, making the top end just under 5cm (2in) across. Then draw a wide border all around this outline. Use the pattern to cut the shape from wrapping paper. Cut an inverted 'V' through the pointed end of the border up to the point of the tie. Fold the borders over, trimming off any excess paper.

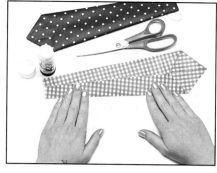

Fold under the top of the tie to hide the cut edge. Cut another piece of paper 10cm x 6cm (4in x 2½in). Fold in the long edges to meet, and wrap the band around the top of the tie. Firmly crease the folds on each side.

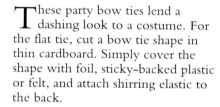

Now remove this piece and pierce a hole in the middle of each crease. Thread a piece of shirring elastic through the hole as shown; the elastic should fit comfortably around the neck. Knot the ends of the elastic, then glue the 'knot' to the tie, with the cut edges stuck down at the back.

These party bow ties lend a dashing look to a costume. For the flat tie, cut a bow tie shape in thin cardboard. Simply cover the shape with foil, sticky-backed plastic or felt, and attach shirring elastic to the back.

Or make a soft fabric tie by cutting a strip of felt or other material 18cm (7in) square. Fold it in half, right sides together, and sew the long edges together to make a tube. Turn it right side out, and finish the raw edges by turning them in and slip-stitching them.

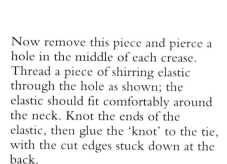

Cut another strip of material 5cm x 9cm (2in x 3½in). Fold the long edges in to meet at the back and glue them down. Wrap this piece around the middle of the tube and sew it in place at the back, folding in the raw edges to hide them. Sew on shirring elastic for wearing the bow.

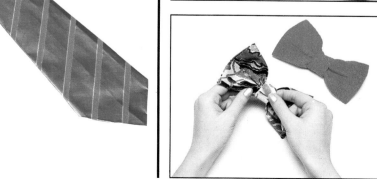

If the day outside is gloomy,
try brightening the outlook
with some 'stained glass window'
pictures. These are cut from black art
paper and backed with coloured
tissue. First cut pieces of art paper 38
by 30cm (15 by 12in). Mark a 3.5cm
(1½in) border all the way round.
Now draw your design, taking care
that it is always connected in some
way to the outer border.

Next cut away any parts of the
picture that you want to be coloured,
taking care not to detach the black
areas from the frame.

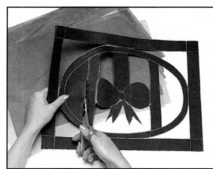

Now glue tissue paper to the back.
For your first attempt use just one
colour; then as you feel more
confident, you can build up pictures
using three or more different coloured
tissues. When the picture is finished,
affix it lightly to the windowpane,
then watch what happens when the
light shines through it.

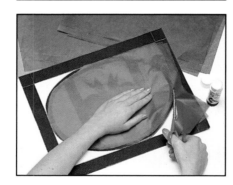

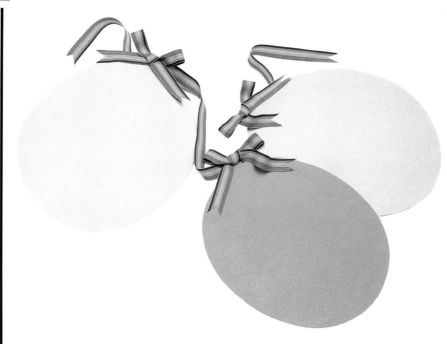

These are just as colourful
as real balloons, but they won't
pop, or even gently expire! Cut out
balloon shapes from coloured
cardboard or stiff paper, then cover
them on one side with spray-on
glitter.

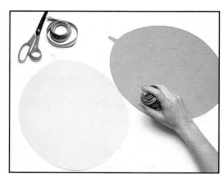

Two balloon shapes can be glued
together at the edges, or they can all
be strung up separately. Tape the
balloons to a length of colourful
striped ribbon.

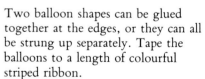

Lastly, use more of the same ribbon
to make up some bows, and fix them
to the balloons with some double-
sided tape.

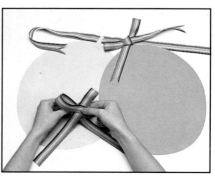

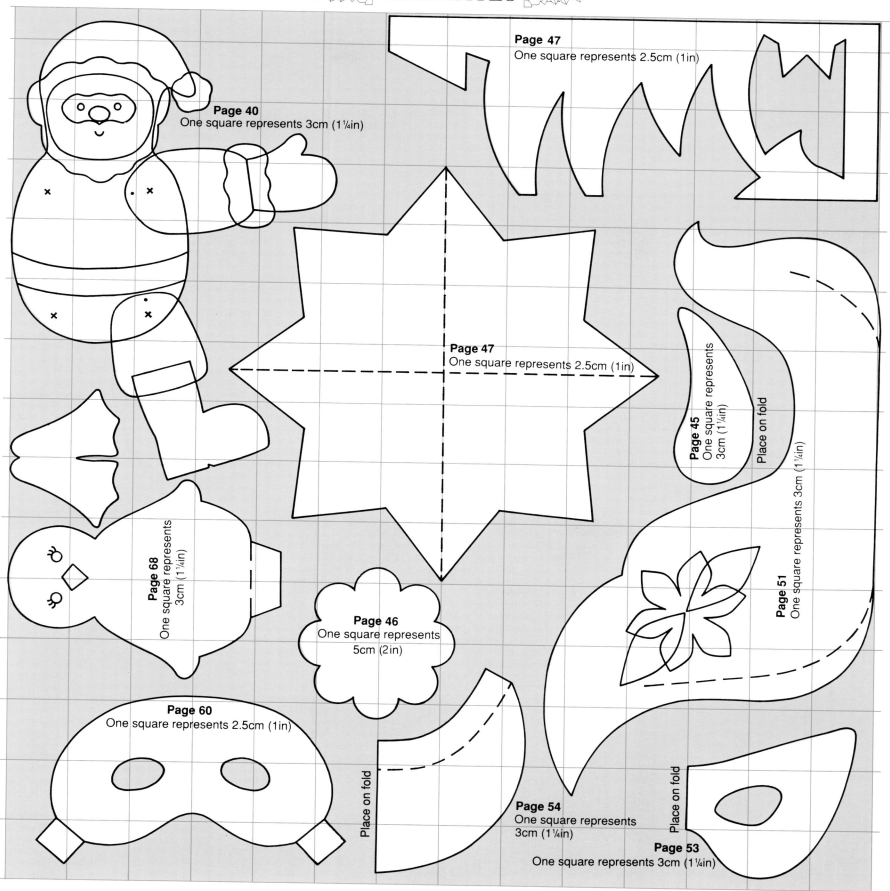

Page 40
One square represents 3cm (1¼in)

Page 47
One square represents 2.5cm (1in)

Page 47
One square represents 2.5cm (1in)

Page 45
One square represents 3cm (1¼in)

Place on fold

Page 51
One square represents 3cm (1¼in)

Page 68
One square represents 3cm (1¼in)

Page 46
One square represents 5cm (2in)

Page 60
One square represents 2.5cm (1in)

Place on fold

Page 54
One square represents 3cm (1¼in)

Place on fold

Page 53
One square represents 3cm (1¼in)

Make that dinner or tea party extra special by creating table decorations in your own style, either to complement your china, the meal itself or simply the occasion. On the following pages you will find a range of ideas to transform your table. As the table centrepiece is often the most important feature we have included a number of beautiful and artistic designs. There are also clever and zany place cards to guide your guests to their seats, crackers for little take-home gifts, co-ordinating place settings as well as novel suggestions for prettying up plain napkins.

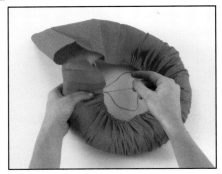

Adorn the New Year dinner table with this attractive centrepiece. Cut a length of magenta crepe paper 120cm x 20cm (48in x 8in). Stick the ends together on the wrong side with clear sticky tape. Place a 25cm (10in) diameter polystyrene ring in the middle and sew the long edges of crepe paper together with a running stitch, enclosing the polystyrene ring. Gather up the seam and fasten off.

Spray five candle holders white and push into the ring, evenly spaced apart. Then drape strings of white pearls and narrow green coiled gift wrapping ribbon around the ring, gluing the ends to the underside.

Stick two rectangles of metallic blue cardboard back to back with spray adhesive and cut out five masks using the template on page 59. Score gently along the fold line of the tabs and bend the tabs backwards. Stick each mask, by the tabs, in front of a candle. Decorate the ring with blue and green star-shaped sequins and silver stars cut from cardboard.

Exquisite marzipan fruits deserve special presentation. Nestling in little tissue 'parcels' and piled into a cake stand, they make a colourful centrepiece. All you need is several different colours of tissue paper and some pinking shears. Instead of marzipan fruits, you could use chocolates or marrons glacés.

Believe it or not, this arrangement is quite simple once you get the hang of folding the cones. You need two colours of foil paper. Cut out lots of boat shapes 16.5cm (6½in) along the top and 12.5 (5in) along the bottom and about 6cm (2½in) deep. Glue one colour to another, back-to-back.

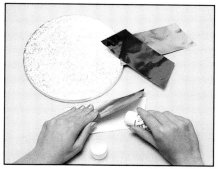

From a double layer of one colour of tissue, cut a 10cm (4in) square. Pinking shears give an attractive serrated edge. From another colour of tissue, also double, cut a smaller square, measuring about 6cm (2½in).

Form each boat into a cone and glue it in place. The first few you make may not look too professional, but it doesn't matter; these can go on the outside of the stand and will be partially covered. You will soon get the hang of folding the cones. Bend the bottoms under; it helps to hold the shape and looks tidier.

Lay the smaller square on top of the larger one. Place the marzipan fruit in the centre and gather the tissue around it. Hold it in place for a few seconds and then let go; the crumpled tissue will retain its rosette shape. Place several of the parcels on a doily-lined glass or china cake stand.

When you have several cones made, start gluing them around the edge of a 20cm- (8in-) diameter silver cake board. Place another two layers inside the first, leaving room for a chunky candle in the middle.

This beautiful cracker is not designed to be pulled but to be taken home as a memento. First take a tube of cardboard and wrap white crepe paper around it. Insert short cardboard tubes into each end, leaving gaps of 5cm (2in) between the main and end sections. Cover the central and end sections on the outside with silver foil paper, and stick pink foil paper to the inside of the end sections.

Wind a length of silver sequin waste around the centre. Next take two strips of pink net and draw a piece of thread through the centre of each to gather it. Tie them at each end with a strip of curling gift wrap ribbon. (Curl the ribbon by running the blunt edge of a pair of scissors along it.)

Finish by decorating the cracker with large sequins and a pink foil heart, or with some other shape if you prefer. If you like, pop a little gift inside — a hand-made chocolate, perhaps, or even a diamond ring!

Make some spring flowers that will bloom throughout the year. For the base of each daffodil head, cut a section from an egg box and trim it down to an even edge. Use a yellow one if you can, or else paint it yellow. Next take a flexible paper or plastic straw and roll it in a strip of green tissue, gluing both long edges. Trim the ends and bend the straw without tearing the paper.

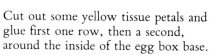

Cut out some yellow tissue petals and glue first one row, then a second, around the inside of the egg box base.

Finally, scrunch up a small piece of orange tissue paper and glue it to the centre of the flower.

What could be prettier than this profusion of ribbons and flowers? The one shown is pink and white, but you should choose whatever matches your décor. First of all you will need a biscuit or cake tin. Cover the outside with silver foil paper, allowing a little extra at the top to turn over and glue. (This will be easier if you snip down to the tin.) Decorate it with strips of ribbon.

Take a block of florists' foam and cut it to fit inside the tin, using the extra bits to fill in the gaps around it.

Now wire up pieces of gift wrap ribbon, little baubles, strips of crepe paper and silk flowers. Curl the ribbon by running the blunt edge of a pair of scissors along it. Push the wires into the foam, arranging them until the tin is totally full. Use strips of ribbon around the outside, and let them fall over the side of the tin.

This collage place card can be made from wrapping paper and scraps of plain stiff paper. Select a gift-wrapping paper with a design that is appropriate to the theme of your party and plain paper in a harmonizing colour. Cut a rectangle of the plain paper about 14 by 9cm (5½ by 3½in) and fold it in half as shown.

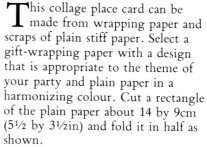

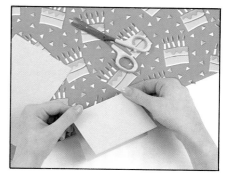

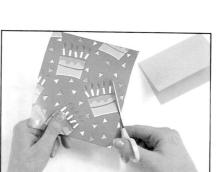

Cut around the shape you have decided to use and stick this to the card with double-sided tape or glue.

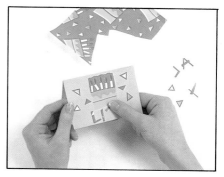

Stick additional shapes onto the card as desired. Put double-sided tape onto the back of a small area of the wrapping paper, and cut thin strips with which to make up the names. Peel off the backing and attach the strips to the card to form the letters.

Make cocktail glasses look extra smart with this chequered place card. First cut a 7.5cm (3in) square from a piece of stiff white cardboard. Use a pencil and ruler to mark off 2.5cm (1in) divisions and join these up to form a grid. Colour in alternate squares with a black felt pen to give a chequerboard pattern.

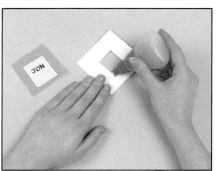

On a 5cm (2in) square of cardboard write the name. Cut out a 6cm (2½in)-square piece of pink net fabric; set it aside. Using a sharp craft knife, cut out the centre of the chequered card to leave a hole 2.5cm (1in) square. Turn the card over and apply some glue around the edges of the hole.

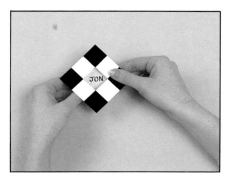

Place the piece of net over the card with the name, and hold them together in one hand while positioning the chequered card diagonally over the top. Press firmly to apply the glue to all three surfaces. Leave the card to dry for a few minutes.

This unusual placemat is easily made from cardboard and a wallpaper border. A black and white border has been chosen here, but you can use a colour which co-ordinates with your table setting. Cut a 30cm (12in) square from a sheet of thick cardboard, using a steel rule and craft knife to ensure precision.

Cut the border into four strips, allowing a little extra on each strip for trimming. Apply double-sided tape to the back of each strip, but do not peel off the protective backing yet. Lay two adjacent strips in place; where they meet at the corners, try to match the pattern repeat. Holding one strip on top of the other, cut diagonally across the corner.

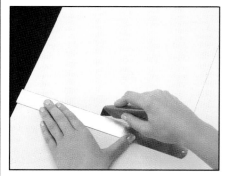

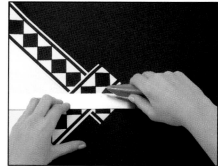

Holding each strip in place along its inner edge, begin to peel back the protective paper from the double-sided tape, as shown. Rub a soft cloth along the border as you peel to stick it in place.

HARLEQUIN PARTY MASK

These unusual harlequin masks form the perfect party centre-piece, especially when co-ordinated with a black and white table setting, as shown on page 64. The masks can be bought or home-made from papier mâché. Paint each mask white.

With a pencil draw diagonal lines across the mask to create a grid. Don't worry if the squares are not exactly symmetrical. Paint alternate squares black.

Glue a length of black lace or net around the edge of the mask. Add coloured feathers and ribbons for the finishing touches. Stand the masks back to back so that one is facing each side of the table.

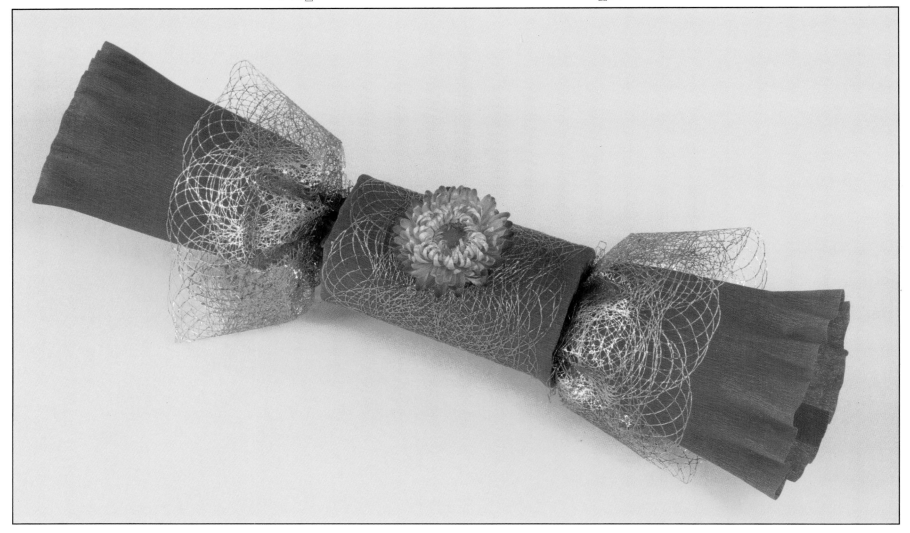

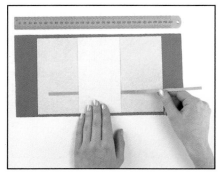

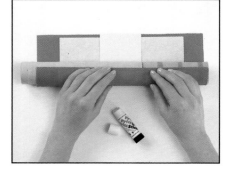

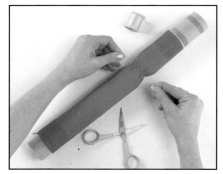

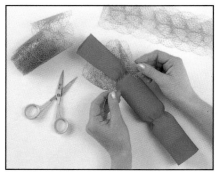

It is easy and economical to make crackers. Cut crepe paper 32cm x 16cm (12³/₄in x 6¹/₄in), keeping the grain of the paper parallel with the long sides. Lay a piece of thin writing paper 24cm x 15cm (9¹/₂in x 6in) centrally on top. Next cut thin cardboard 15cm x 8cm (6in x 3in) and lay it across the centre. Slip a cracker snap underneath.

Take two cardboard tubes, the sort found inside rolls of kitchen towel, and cut one in half. Lay the long tube on the lower edge of the crepe paper, with the end level with the cardboard edge. Butt a short tube against the long one and roll up tightly. Glue the overlapped edges of paper together with a low-tack adhesive.

Pull the short tube out for 5cm (2in) and tie thread tightly around the cracker between the tubes. Push the tubes together again then remove the short tube. Drop a gift, motto and paper hat inside and pull out the long tube a further 12.5cm (5in) . Tie thread tightly between the tube and cardboard inside the cracker. Untie the threads.

Cut two 25cm (10in) lengths of gold filigree lace – the kind that has a drawstring thread along one edge. Gather up the drawstring and tie the lace around the necks of the cracker. Gently stretch the ends of the cracker to flute the edge. Remove the drawstring from a length of lace and glue around the middle of the cracker. Glue a dried flower head in place to complete.

VINE GARLAND CANDLE RING

Gold and silver look stunning by candlelight and this festive arrangement will flatter any table setting. To begin, spray a vine garland with gold paint, sprinkle with gold glitter, and leave to dry.

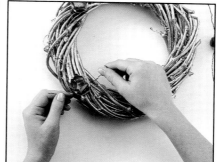

Take three flat-based candle holders and stick florists' fixative putty under each one. Position them evenly-spaced around the garland using florists' wire to secure each holder firmly in place. To make the silver roses – four for each candle – cut strips of silver crepe paper 53cm (21in) long and 9cm (3½in) wide. Fold the strips in half lengthways and tuck the short ends in.

Run a strip of double-sided tape along the lower edge of a folded strip, and place a wired group of small gold balls at one end. Roll the crepe paper around the balls, removing the tape's backing paper as you go and pinching the paper tightly together at the base. When you have finished rolling, crimp the petal edges to curve outwards.

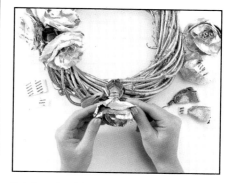

Stick a double-sided adhesive pad to the base of each rose and position four flowers around each candle holder. Cut 23cm (9in) lengths of gold ribbon and fold into double loops. Secure the ends with florists' wire and stick between the roses using adhesive pads. Tease the rose petals and gold loops into shape to hide the holders, and put candles in place.

Miniature holly sprigs give a festive touch to a place card. From thin cardboard cut a rectangle 7.5cm x 10cm (3in x 4in). Gently score across the centre, using a craft knife against a ruler, and fold the card in half. Punch a hole in the lower left side. Make a holly leaf template from thick paper and draw around the edge on to thick green paper (artist's Canson paper is ideal). Cut out.

Score lightly down the centre of each leaf and bend to shape. Bind a bunch of red flower stamens (available from craft shops) together with fine florists' wire and cut in half across the stems to create two bunches. Bind the stamens to the front of the leaves with red florists' tape.

Fold a short length of narrow curling ribbon in half, at a slight angle, and secure fold with a small piece of double-sided tape. Curl the ribbon against a scissor blade and stick to the front of the holly sprig. Write the name on the card and push the holly sprig through the punched hole, securing the stems to the back of the card with a small piece of sticky tape.

These cheerful chicks will guide guests to their seats for Easter tea. Use template on page 59 to cut out a chick in lemon coloured cardboard and a beak and feet in orange cardboard. Glue the beak to the chick and draw the eyes with a black felt-tipped pen.

Write the name of your guest with a pencil diagonally on the chick using a letter stencil. Fill in the letters with a felt-tipped pen.

Score along the broken lines on the chick and bend the tab backwards at a right angle. Glue the tab to the chick's feet.

These colourful place cards are perfect for a children's party. For each kite you will need stiff paper in two colours. From each colour cut two rectangles, each 10 by 15cm (4 by 6in). Draw a line down the centre, then another line at right angles across it, 5cm (2in) from one end. Join up the points, then cut off the four corners; set them aside.

Use two of the corners of the red card to decorate the yellow kite, glueing them in place as shown. Similarly, use two of the leftover pieces of the yellow card to decorate the red kite. Write the name on each kite.

Cut out squares of coloured tissue, allowing three for each kite. On the back of each kite, glue a 40cm (16in) strip of thin ribbon. Pinch the squares of tissue together in the centre and tie the ribbon around them. Cut a small strip of cardboard, fold it in two and glue it to the back of the kite; use this hook to attach the kite to a glass.

This original place card is simple to make using different colours of stiff paper and scraps of net. First cut a rectangle out of lightweight cardboard, twice the depth of the finished card; fold it in half. Using a craft knife and a steel ruler, cut sections of the card away to create an irregular edge. The cards can be any shape; in fact, it is more fun if they all look a little different.

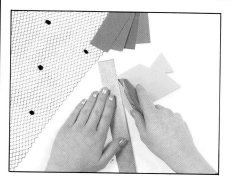

From the coloured paper cut the letters to spell each guest's name. Don't try to cut rounded shapes, as this is more difficult. It may be easier to make some letters from two pieces. For a letter A, for example, cut a V shape, turn it upside down, and add a separate strip for the crossbar. Glue the letters in place.

Cut irregular pieces from a scrap of net, and lightly glue these in place over the name. Place each card on a plate on top of a folded napkin, as shown.

Quick and easy to make, this place mat will brighten up the supper table. Cut a wavy-edged rectangle of blue cardboard 35cm x 25cm (14in x 10in). Cut a row of wavy slits lengthwise across the mat with a craft knife.

This sparkling placemat is an obvious winner for Christmas. First draw a Christmas tree on the reverse (matt) side of a piece of shiny green cardboard. The length should be about 10cm (4in) longer than the diameter of your dinner plate and the width about 20cm (8in) wider. Cut out the mat using a craft knife and a steel ruler.

Cut wavy-edged strips 23cm (9in) long from green cardboard. Weave the first strip in and out of the slits close to one end. Weave in the remaining strips starting each alternate strip at the next slit up.

Add 'ornaments' by sticking tiny baubles to the tips of the tree using strong glue.

On the back, lift up the ends of the strips and glue to the mat. Make a matching coaster from a small wavy-edged square of cardboard.

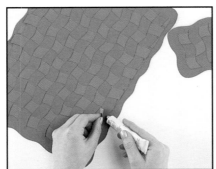

Cut out or buy a star shape to put at the top of the tree. Finally, stick small silver stars over the mat. Or, if you prefer, just scatter the stars freely over the mat, first positioning each mat on the table.

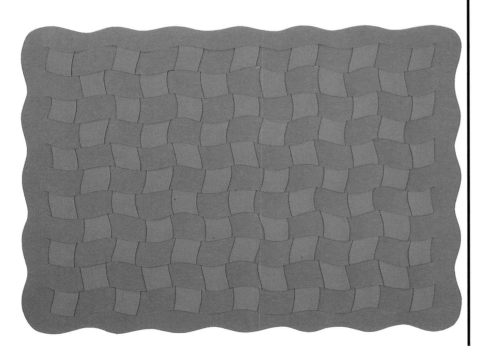

Christmas colours are woven together to make a matching table mat and napkin set. From cartridge paper cut out a

rectangle 37cm x 27cm (14½in x 10½in) and mark a 2.5cm (1in) border all round. Draw lines 12mm (½in) apart across the paper. Cut a piece of sticky-backed velour fabric a little larger all round and peel off the backing paper. Lay the rectangle centrally on top and, using a craft knife, cut through the drawn lines as shown. Fold overlapping fabric over and stick down.

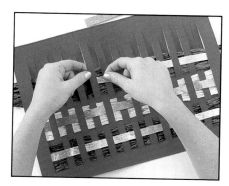

Weave lengths of green and white paper rope through the cut stripes, arranging the ribbon so both ends pass under the border. Fold gold and silver crepe paper into narrow strips and weave over the green and white ribbon. Hold the strips in place with double-sided tape at both ends. Trim away the excess paper, then cut a piece of fabric to cover the back of the mat.

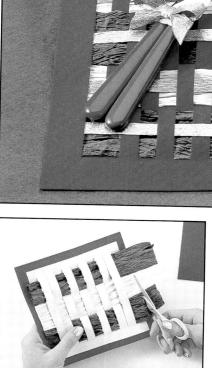

Cut a coaster mat from cartridge paper 17cm (6½in) square. Make a border as for the table mat, and mark, cover and cut in the same way. Weave with two lengths of each colour and cover the back with sticky-backed fabric as before.

To make the napkin ring, cut a strip from cartridge paper 17cm x 6.5cm (6½in x 2½in). Mark out a 12mm (½in) border and divide into strips 12mm (½in) apart. Cover with sticky-backed fabric, and cut strips as before. Weave green ribbon and silver or gold crepe through the slits and secure with double-sided tape. Cut a length of fabric for the backing and stick in place.

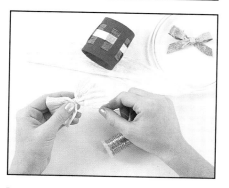

Join the two ends of the ring by overlapping them and securing with double-sided tape. Make a bow shape from white paper ribbon, binding the centre with fine florists' wire. Make a small bow shape from folded gold crepe paper and stick across the white bow with double-sided tape. Stick the completed bow across the join in the napkin ring using double-sided tape.

Here's a quick and simple way to dress up a plain napkin for afternoon tea. All you need is a square paper doily, preferably in a colour contrasting with the napkin, and a floral motif. Begin by folding the napkin into a triangle.

Fold the doily diagonally. To create a 'spine' to allow for the thickness of the napkin, unfold the doily and make another crease about 1cm (^{3}/8in) from the first fold.

Cut out a Victorian scrap or other floral motif and glue it to the centre of the smaller (top) side of the doily. Insert the napkin.

Here are a couple of ideas for jazzing up ordinary paper napkins. For the blue napkin, cut a star shape from a piece of cardboard — the cardboard must be slightly wider than the folded napkin. Hold the cardboard firmly in place over the napkin and spray silver or gold paint over the area. Let the paint dry for several minutes before you allow anything else to touch it.

The white napkins have a design stencilled on them with oil-based stencil crayons. You can buy these separately or in packs, with ready-cut stencils. Choose your design, then place it over the area you want to stencil — in this case the corner of the napkin. Rub the crayon over a spare area of stencil, then take the colour up onto the brush and paint it over the stencil, in a circular motion.

Use the brush only over the parts you wish to show up in that colour. Now switch to the next colour. It is best to use a different brush for each colour if you want clear colour definition.

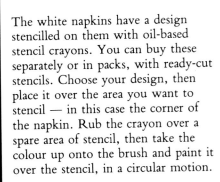

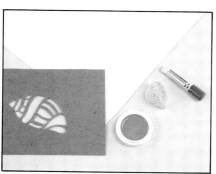

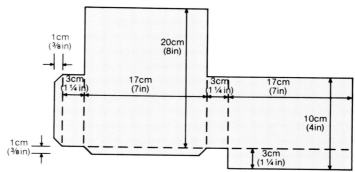

A nother stencilled napkin, this time to co-ordinate with your china or decorative scheme. All you need is a plain napkin – a stencil motif – either bought (quilters' suppliers have them) or original, a natural sponge and some fabric paint.

Potision the stencil on the napkin. Mix the paint in a saucer or palette. Dip the sponge into the paint and dab it on a piece of scrap paper to remove the excess. As an alternative to a sponge you can use a stencil brush, which will give a slightly different effect. It is worthwhile trying both to see which best suits your design.

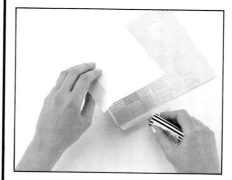

T o make this attractive napkin box, draw the above diagram to the measurements indicated. Cut it out with a sharp knife and score the folds marked with a dotted line. Cut out a piece of water-resistant paper or PVC, approximately 21cm x 19cm (8½in by 7½in). Stick it down onto the front inside area of the box, and fold overlapping paper to the back of the card; glue it in place.

You can either hold the stencil in place with your fingers or fasten it with tape. Dab paint through the stencil onto the fabric, taking care that it doesn't seep under the edges. When the paint is dry, fix it following the manufacturer's instructions.

Apply glue to the sides and base of the box and stick the box together. Cut out a second piece of paper 26cm x 12.5cm (10½in by 5in) and glue it onto the outside front and sides of the box, snipping the corners to enable you to tuck the free edges in. Finally, cut a third piece of paper 20cm x 17cm (8in x 7in) to glue to the back of the box and cover all the untidy edges.

Throughout the year, there are many anniversaries and important dates that you will want to celebrate by giving a present or sending a greeting card. A personalized gift wrap adds a touch of class to a gift. This section shows how to decorate your own paper by stencilling and marbling. There are also ideas for making gift tags and cards for many occasions, plus containers to hold that special gift such as the parcel disguised as a train or the paisley gift pouch. And if you are too busy to make your own gift wrap, there are some very quick and simple ideas for decorating a plainly wrapped present.

Create your own personalized gift wrap by stencilling onto plain paper. Draw a simple motif on cardboard to use as a template and cut it out. Trace around the motif at random on stencil board.

Use a craft knife and a cutting board to cut out the stencil shapes. Place the stencil over the paper and hold in place with masking tape.

Tape scraps of the stencil board over some of the cut-outs. Spray evenly over the stencil with gold spray paint. When the paint is dry uncover the other stencils and cover the painted ones. Now spray with silver spray paint. Leave to dry.

GIFT BOX ROSETTE

FAN TOPPED GIFTBOX

Y‌ou will need the type of gift wrap ribbon which sticks to itself when moistened for this decoration. First cut two strips of ribbon at least 40cm (16in) long. Twist each piece into a figure-of-eight, moistening the ends to hold in place. Stick one piece at right angles over the other. Repeat with two more strips 5cm (2in) shorter.

Stick the second rosette on top of the first. To finish, make a loop out of a short strip of ribbon and stick it in the centre. For a more traditional rosette, simply make the loops shorter and tighter.

A‌ fan adds panache to a plain giftbox. Cut one long edge from a large rectangular paper doily, making it about 7cm (2¾in) deep. Cut cartridge paper a little deeper and wider than this and cover with foil gift wrap using spray adhesive. Glue the doily strip onto one side, cut the top edge following the curves of the doily, then pleat up concertina-style.

Open out the concertina into a fan shape and run a length of double-sided tape along the base to hold it in place. Do not remove the backing paper. From narrow curling ribbon cut five 15cm (6in) lengths, and from foil, five 6cm (2½in) squares. Stick a foil square to the end of each ribbon with double-sided tape and curl the foil around the ribbon. Secure the ends with more tape.

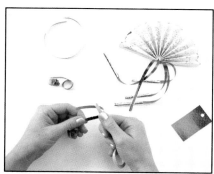

Remove the backing paper from the base of the fan and stick the ribbon ends to the centre. Make a gift tag from a rectangle of paper and cover with foil using spray adhesive. Punch a hole in it, attach a length of gold thread and join to the fan. Curl the ends of three lengths of ribbon and stick them to the front of the fan with PVA glue or tape. Stick the fan diagonally across the gift box.

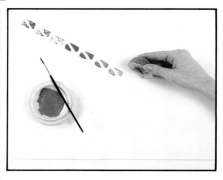

Save the expense of buying wrapping paper by decorating your own. There are many ways to decorate papers: this design is a simple potato print. Cut the potato in half and then sculpt it with a sharp knife so that your motif stands proud. Apply paint to the motif with a brush and then print the colour on to the paper, creating a regular pattern. Re-apply the paint as necessary.

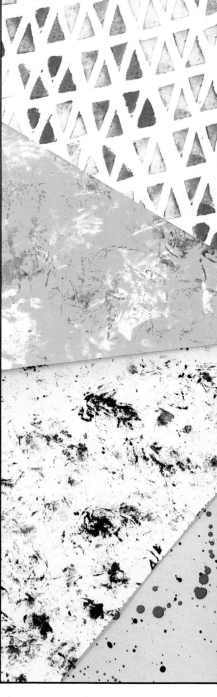

Gift wrapping can prove so expensive these days, so why not make your own gift boxes? Here, some plain cardboard boxes have been covered in hand-marbled paper. Fill a large bowl with water, then mix some solvent-based paint such as ceramic paint, or some artist's oil colours, with a little white spirit. Use a paint brush to drop successive colours on to the surface of the water.

Stir the mixture with the handle of your paint brush or an old stick until you have a pleasant swirling pattern. An alternative way to form a pattern is to blow the paint across the surface of the water.

This design is done by ragging. Pour the paint into a container and dip a soft cloth into it. Dab off any excess paint on to waste paper, then apply the first colour in a random manner. Repeat the procedure with a second and even a third colour.

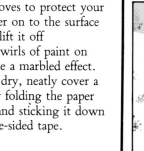

Wearing rubber gloves to protect your hands, put the paper on to the surface of the water, then lift it off immediately. The swirls of paint on the paper will create a marbled effect. When the paper is dry, neatly cover a small box, carefully folding the paper round the corners and sticking it down with glue or double-sided tape.

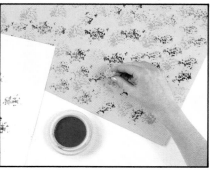

This paper is decorated by sponging, first with gold paint, then with a mid blue and finally with pink. Pour some paint into a container and dip a small natural sponge lightly into the paint. Remove any excess paint by dabbing the sponge on to waste paper, then apply the paint to your paper with light dabbing movements.

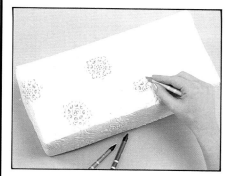

Wallpaper is often useful as a gift covering — particularly if your present is very large. Here we have used thick wallpaper with an embossed pattern and given it a touch of style and individuality. Wrap your gift, and choose some wax crayons in contrasting shades. Rub a colour over the raised surface of the wallpaper to highlight one of the motifs in the design.

Choose another colour, and use it to pick out another section in the pattern. (Instead of wax crayons, you could use coloured pencils or chalk; the latter would need to be rubbed with a tissue afterwards to remove loose dust. The medium you choose must slide over the embossing without colouring in the whole design — paint is therefore not suitable.)

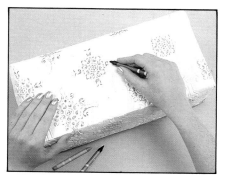

Repeat the process using a third colour and continue with as many shades as you like. A tip while wrapping your gift — you'll probably find that ordinary tape will not stick to the surface of wallpaper; double-sided tape used between two folds will be more effective.

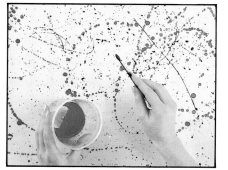

This flicked or splattered design is achieved by flicking paint over the paper. Use a fine brush and flick on the first colour, in this case metallic grey. If you want a variety of marks change the thickness of the brush. Create other designs by drawing wavy lines with felt tip pens, or tracing round a novelty pastry cutter (such as the teddy bear shape above).

CONFETTI CLUSTERS

FANFARE

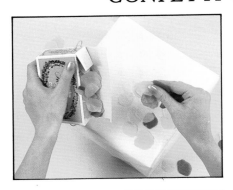

This simple but effective idea is just right for a wedding. Cover your gift with plain paper. Buy some rose petal-shaped confetti. Alternatively, you could make the petals yourself from softly-coloured tissue paper: fold a piece of tissue into about eight and cut out an oval shape; repeat for as many petals as you need.

Arrange a cluster in a flower-shape on each corner of the gift. Stick each petal into position with a small dab of glue right at one end of the petal. When the glue is dry, bend up the petals to give a 3-dimensional effect. You could use this idea for a silver anniversary gift by wrapping the parcel in aluminium foil and using petals of just one colour.

Paper fans are simple to make but can look stunning, used either singly or in a row to create a ruffle around your gift. Cut a strip of paper the width you'd like the fan to be when opened, and three times the length. Fold it in half widthways, then fold it up in small even pleats, starting with the folded end. Get a sharp crease along the pleats by running them firmly between your fingers.

When you have pleated the entire length, hold the pleats together with the folded edge of the strip on top. Bend the fan in half and stick the two folded edges together with sticky tape along their length as shown. Make sure that the tape continues right to the outer edge so that the join cannot be seen when the fan is open.

Open out the fan and apply double-sided tape to its flat side; stick the fan in position on your gift. Care is needed in deciding how big to make the fan — too big and the present will be swamped, too small and it will look insignificant. It might be worthwhile experimenting with rough fans cut from newspaper first, to get the scale right before cutting your gift wrap.

A TISSUE POSY

BORDERLINES

Wallpaper borders can look very effective on any square- or rectangular-shaped gift. Cut a strip of border the length of one side of your wrapped gift; glue it in place along the edge.

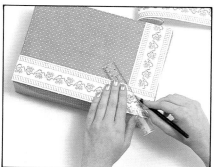

Cut another border strip for an adjacent edge. Apply glue, and position the strip so that the end of it overlaps the first strip. Now mitre the overlapped corners by trimming the top strip at an angle. Do this by ruling a line between the corner of the gift and the point at which the strips overlap, as shown here.

Cut off the excess triangle of wallpaper border with a craft knife. Don't press too hard or you could damage the gift underneath. Cut two matching border strips for the other edges of the gift and repeat the mitring process with the remaining three corners.

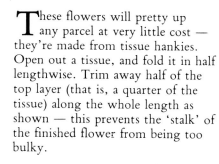

These flowers will pretty up any parcel at very little cost — they're made from tissue hankies. Open out a tissue, and fold it in half lengthwise. Trim away half of the top layer (that is, a quarter of the tissue) along the whole length as shown — this prevents the 'stalk' of the finished flower from being too bulky.

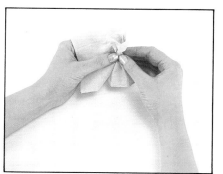

Tuck in the top corner of one end very slightly and gather up the tissue in very small pleats, gradually turning the 'flower' round as you go. When the gathering is completed, fold in the top corner of the end of the tissue as before.

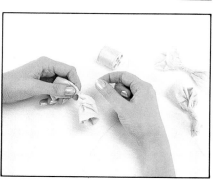

Give the 'stalk' a couple of twists to make it firm. Bind it tightly with thread and tie it securely. Make as many flowers as you need for your gift — you can make an entire bouquet if you like and wrap it up in a paper doily. Tie the flowers together with a ribbon, make a bow and attach the bouquet to your present.

Brightly-coloured drinking straws lend themselves to decorating presents. Look for colours to co-ordinate with your gift wrap. The straws can be made of paper or plastic; both work well. Select the colours you want and cut four straws in half; discard one of each half. Cut another four straws in two, leaving one section slightly longer than the other; retain both pieces.

Place four halves, one of each colour, together over a central point in a star shape and staple them together. Do the same with the other slightly longer straws and their shorter counterparts so that you end up with three stars of slightly different sizes. With the smallest on top and largest on the bottom, staple all three together. Attach the triple star to the parcel with double-sided tape.

Brightly-coloured adhesive tape can give any plain wrapping paper a touch of style. A geometric design is easiest to create with tape, and the most effective; curves are rather difficult! Work out your design first and measure it out accurately on the parcel in pencil.

Stick the tapes in place along the pencil marks. Take care that the tapes don't stretch at all during application or they will cause the paper to pucker slightly. Sticky tapes are available in an enormous variety of colours, textures and patterns; choose a strong contrast with your paper.

The delicate silhouette of a doily against a contrasting background colour looks attractive on a gift. Wrap your present up in plain paper and glue the doilies wherever you like. To decorate the corners of a large gift, fold a doily in half, then in half again.

Unfold the doily carefully and spread it out. Cut off one of the quarters of the doily; the folds along which you should cut will be clearly visible.

Paste the doily over one corner of the gift as shown. Repeat with alternate corners, unless your gift has enough space to take a doily over each corner without overlap. The doilies don't have to be white: silver or gold is also effective. Nor do they have to be circular — square ones would be smart on a square-sided present.

Use a sophisticated print like a paisley design to set off this pouch which is ideal for holding a small gift. Apply gift wrap to one side of thin cardboard with spray glue. Use the template on page 95 to cut out two pouches and mark the position of the holes and broken lines. Cut the tabs off one pouch and punch holes on the other one.

Score both pouches along the broken lines on the right side and fold the tabs backwards. Stick the pouches together with double-sided tape on the tabs.

These rigid little boxes are ideal for presenting jewellery but you can make them to fit anything you like. Choose thin cardboard, either in the colour you want the finished box to be, or white so that you can cover it later with gift wrap. Measure out the template on page 95. The size of the triangular sides doesn't matter, as long as they are all the same, and the base is a true square.

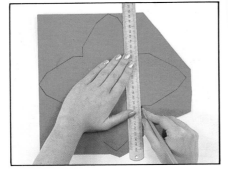

Thread cord through the holes and knot the ends inside. To close the pouch hold the sides between your thumb and finger and gently squeeze the pouch open. Now press down one of the ellipses. Close the other ellipse on top.

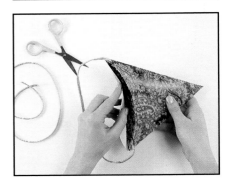

Cut out along the exterior lines with a craft knife. If you're covering the cardboard shape with gift wrap, do it at this stage, cutting the paper to fit. Score along all the fold lines carefully, using the back of the craft knife, then bend the box along the score marks, creasing firmly.

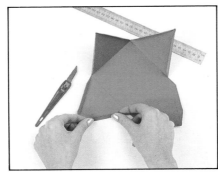

Punch holes in each apex and fold the box into its pyramidal shape. Thread the ribbon in and out of the four holes and, making sure all the side-folds are tucked inside the box, tie the loose ends together with a bow.

This elegant little box is ideal for wrapping a special gift. First draw the diagram to the specified measurements, then trace it. Tape the tracing to the wrong side of medium-weight cardboard with masking tape and draw over the outline with a ballpoint pen to make a light indentation in the cardboard. Cut around the outline.

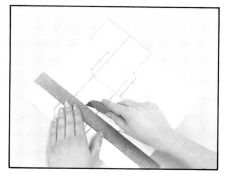

Score the fold lines carefully with scissor points and fold the box accordingly. Apply glue to the flaps and join the box together as shown. Allow it to dry thoroughly before using it.

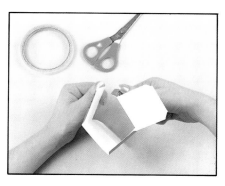

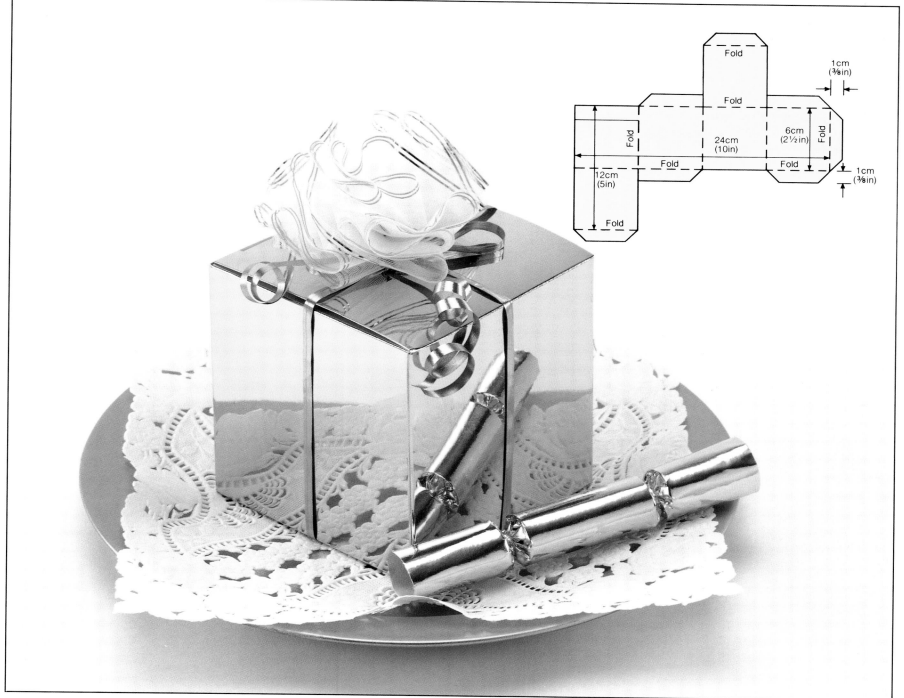

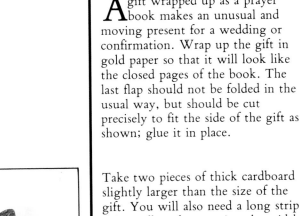

A gift wrapped up as a prayer book makes an unusual and moving present for a wedding or confirmation. Wrap up the gift in gold paper so that it will look like the closed pages of the book. The last flap should not be folded in the usual way, but should be cut precisely to fit the side of the gift as shown; glue it in place.

Take two pieces of thick cardboard slightly larger than the size of the gift. You will also need a long strip of thin cardboard measuring the width and length of the gift. Use tape to stick the thick cardboard on to either side of the thin cardboard to make a book cover for the gift. Cover the outside with plain paper as shown; glue all the edges down firmly.

A smartly-dressed present for a smartly-dressed man — or woman! This is suitable for a tall thin gift. Wrap it up in paper of a colour and design that is plausible for a shirt. Cut out a 'collar' shape as shown from stiff white paper; fix it in position around the top of the parcel with glue or double-sided tape.

Using patterned ribbon for the tie (such as this elegant paisley design), wrap it around the collar and knot it like a tie. Before pulling it tight, put some glue or double-sided tape on the collar where the tie should sit; position the tie correctly and tighten the knot. Finally, fold over the two corners of the collar shape to make an elegantly formal shirt; make sure the collar is even.

Spread glue over the inside of the book cover, and place the gift firmly on one side of it. Wrap the cover over the other side of the gift, making sure it's stuck properly. Cut out gold crosses (or other appropriate symbols relevant for your recipient's religion) and stick them in place. This idea is also good for a christening or anniversary gift.

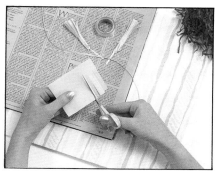

Disguise the unmistakable shape of a record by making it look like a cushion. First create paper tassels. Cut a piece of coloured paper into narrow strips leaving about 2.5cm (1in) at the bottom uncut so that you create a fringe. Roll up the fringe, catching in a short length of narrow ribbon. Secure the tassel with coloured tape.

Take some wrapping paper that is more than twice the size of the gift, fold it in half around the record and cut it so that it is just a little larger. Join two of the sides together with coloured tape along their full length, attaching the ends of the tassels at the corners as you do so. Put a strip of tape over the folded edge of the 'bag'.

Stuff the inside of the 'bag' on both sides of the record with shredded tissue, being careful to put some in the corners. Don't use too much or the wrapping paper will wrinkle. Seal along the remaining open edge with tape.

Any little girl would be thrilled if her present looked like a hat. This idea obviously will only work on a gift that is circular and flat, so that the gift itself can form the crown. Cut a brim from a circle of thin cardboard and cover it with a circle of plain, pastel-coloured paper. Wrap the present by rolling it in matching paper, as shown.

Make sure the paper fits tightly around the base by folding it in a series of small triangles. Trim the turning on the top of the gift to leave a small edge; fold that in neat triangles too. Stick the triangles down on to each other with tape, making sure that the surface is left as flat as possible.

Place the gift in the centre of the brim and stick it in position with glue or double-sided tape. Cut another circle of wrapping paper slightly smaller than the diameter of the crown; glue it in place. Tie a ribbon around the junction of the crown and brim, leaving the ends trailing. Cut a 'V' in the ribbon ends and glue on a couple of artificial flowers for a finishing touch.

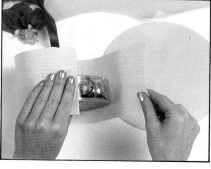

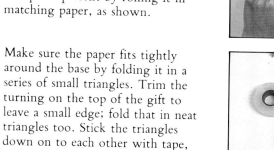

LET'S GO FLY A KITE

Here's another clever idea for disguising a record. Get two large squares of cardboard; the side of a box will do. Position the record in one corner as shown and draw a line from the bottom right corner of the record to the top right corner of the cardboard. Draw a second rule from the top left corner of the record to complete the kite shape. Repeat for the other square.

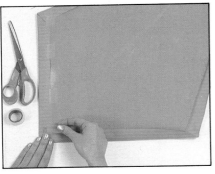

Cut out the shapes and sandwich the record between them. Cover one side in coloured paper, folding over the edges and fixing them with sticky tape on the reverse. Cut another piece of paper slightly smaller than the cardboard shape; glue it in position on the back of the kite.

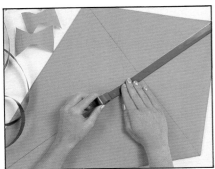

Draw two lines joining the four corners of the kite, and put contrasting tape along them; take care not to stretch the tape as it will pucker the paper. Cut out as many paper bow shapes as you want for the kite's tail. Attach the bows with double-sided tape or glue to a length of ribbon and stick the tail in position behind the longest point of the kite.

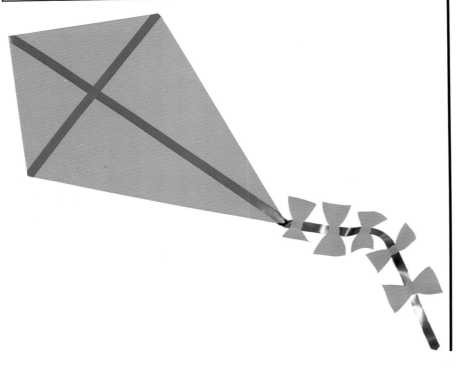

CHRISTMAS CHEER

Bottles of seasonal spirits make an ideal present — but hide such an obvious-looking gift under the decorative guise of a Christmas tree. Find a flower-pot just big enough to take the base of the bottle. From thin cardboard cut out a third section of a large circle and make a deep cone about 8cm (3in) shorter than the bottle. Cover the cone with suitable wrapping paper.

Put the bottle in the flower-pot and place the cone on top. You may need to trim the cone if it seems to cover too much of the flower-pot; do this with care, since you could easily make the cone too short! Double over a piece of tinsel, tie it in a knot and stick it on top of the 'tree'.

H ere is a novel way to disguise two lightweight presents. Put each gift in a rectangular box and wrap with giftwrap. Apply double-sided tape to the end of one box (the smallest, if they vary in size). Peel off the tape backing and press the gift against the other one making an 'L' shape.

From mounting board, cut two large circles for the back wheels and two smaller ones for the front. Cut a circle for each wheel in giftwrap with 1.5cm (⅝in) added all around. Stick the wheel on the wrong side and snip into the edge all around. Apply double-sided tape to the circumference of the wheel and stick the snipped edge over onto the tape.

Cut giftwrap circles slightly smaller than the wheels and stick to the wrong side. Use a craft knife to cut a slice from a cardboard tube for the funnel. Apply double-sided tape in a cross shape over one end and remove the backing tape. Roll the funnel in a strip of giftwrap, snip the excess at the top and tuck it inside.

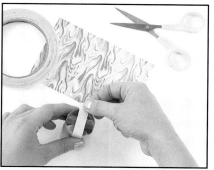

Use a strong glue to stick the wheels to the sides of the train, then press the funnel onto the 'engine'. Stick three lengths of narrow giftwrapping ribbon together at one end. To coil the ribbon, pull the lengths smoothly over the blades of a pair of scissors. Stick the ribbon inside the funnel for the 'smoke'.

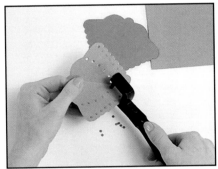

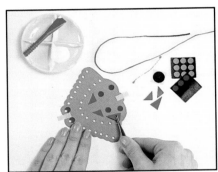

Used greeting cards can often be turned into very acceptable gift tags. Sometimes, as here, the design lends itself to forming a tag. Cut very carefully around the lines of the motif you want to use. Make a hole with a punch, thread a ribbon through the hole and no one would guess the tag had a previous life!

Sometimes a little imagination is needed to give the tag a new and ready-made look. Here, the shape of the tag is outlined on the cardboard in red with a felt-tipped pen. Draw the outline lightly in pencil first to be absolutely sure it is the right size and shape to create the finished label.

Square up the template on page 95 and transfer onto thin cardboard. Place template on card, draw round and cut out. Score and fold along centre. Punch two lines of holes along wings.

Hold butterfly firmly on table with masking tape. With children's stick-on play shapes and stationers' dots, make a pattern on wings. Stick on a large dot for a head and flower stamens, coloured with felt-tipped pen, for antennae. Thread a piece of narrow satin or gift wrap ribbon through holes in wings to attach to a parcel.

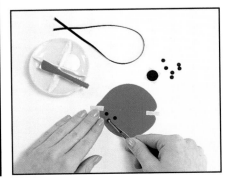

For the ladybird, square up the template on page 95 and transfer onto card. Cut out and score along centre. Hold ladybird flat on table using masking tape. Use black spots, either punched from black paper, sequins, or stationers' dots coloured black. Glue dots randomly. Punch a hole at top of ladybird's wings and thread through narrow black satin ribbon to make a bow.

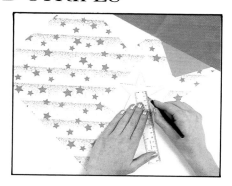

A different way of matching the label to the paper is to create a larger version of a shape which appears in the gift wrap. Begin by drawing a scaled-up shape of the motif from the paper and use it as a template from which to trace the design on to the coloured cardboard.

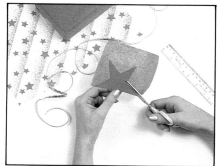

For this idea to be really effective, the colour of the tag should be as close as possible to that in the gift wrap. A layer of tissue laid over the cardboard of a near-match, as shown, might make all the difference to duplicating the final colour. Cut out the shape, and punch a hole to enable you to tie it to the gift.

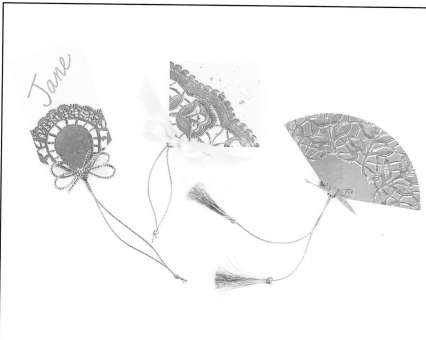

Cut out tags in coloured cardboard or speckled paper. Either cut a single tag and write the message on the back or fold the card in half and cut out a double tag where the message will be inside. Cut a section from a gold paper doily and stick it to the front with spray glue. Trim away any excess level with the edges of the tag.

Pierce a hole on a corner of the tag with the points of a pair of scissors. Cut a length of fine gold cord and bend it in half. Insert the ends through the hole and pull through the loop. Knot the cord ends together or sew them to small gold tassels for extra style.

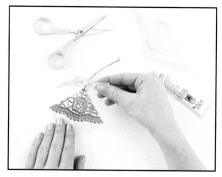

To decorate the tags further you can write the recipient's name in gold pen and glue on a bow.

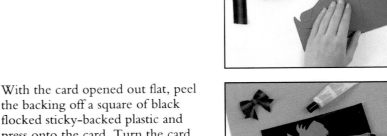

This top dog with a smart tartan bow makes a super greeting card. Cut out a cardboard pattern of the template on page 95 and mark the broken lines. Place the pattern on a 20cm (8in) square of blue cardboard with the lower edges level and the dog's nose against one edge. Draw around the pattern, score along the broken lines and cut along solid lines.

Here is a card that will appeal to cat lovers everywhere. Cut a rectangle of coloured cardboard 26cm x 19.7cm (10¼in x 7¾in). Use the template on page 95 to draw the design on the right-hand side of the card. Score along the broken lines with a craft knife and cut out the long window edge, window panes, cat's eye and the edge of the windowsill.

Fold the card in two along the scored line and trace around the dog on the lower section of the card. Now cut out this dog leaving the fold intact and cutting away the base of the tail in a neat curve.

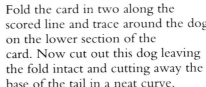

Fold the card in half along the scored line and then open out the inside of the card. Cut a rectangle of pretty wrapping paper measuring 12cm x 6.5cm (4¾in x 2½in). Glue the paper inside the card over the top window panes.

With the card opened out flat, peel the backing off a square of black flocked sticky-backed plastic and press onto the card. Turn the card over and cut around the two Scotties. Fold the card in half and glue a ribbon bow to the front.

POP-OUT SNOWMAN

T here is a surprise for the person who opens this card. Cut a rectangle of blue cardboard 26cm x 21cm (10½in x 8¼in). Score widthwise across the centre and fold in half. Tear white paper into strips and glue across the lower edge on the front and inside. Cut out two green trees from thin cardboard and glue to the front.

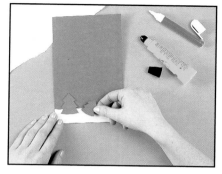

Paint snowflakes with a white typing correction pen. Use the template on page 95 to cut out the snowman in white cardboard, the hat and scarf in yellow and the eyes, nose and buttons in black. Draw a pattern on the scarf and hat with a red pen. Glue all the pieces to the snowman and draw a smile with a black felt-tipped pen.

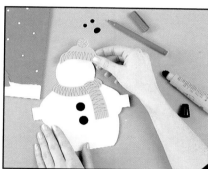

Score along the centre of the snowman and the broken lines on the tabs. Bend the snowman in half along the scored centre and place him inside the card matching the fold to the opening edges of the card and keeping the lower edges level. Glue the tabs inside the card.

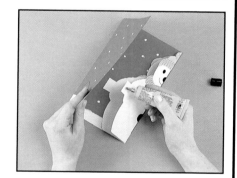

PEACOCK TAILS

G ossamer-fine Japanese paper napkins make quick cards. Simply cut out designs and glue them to cards. With a sharp craft knife, cut a fan shape from a circular peacock napkin, so that the two large 'eyes' are at top. Spray glue back of fan, position and smooth onto card.

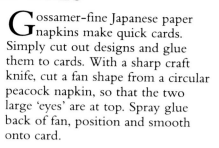
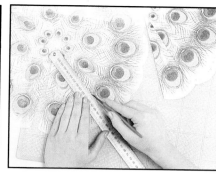

Cut two further eyes from napkin. Arrange, spray glue wrong side and smooth down onto card.

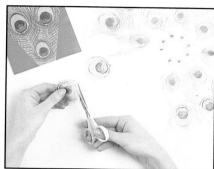

Experiment with different designs and cards to highlight the subtle colours. Butterflies on gold make an exotic card.

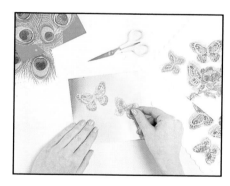

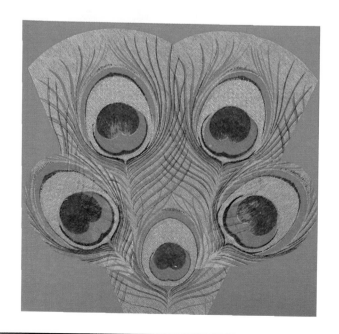

Making use of a ready-printed design gives a very professional finish, as you can see on this 3-D greetings card. Choose a pack of notelets or sheet of giftwrap with a detailed repeat motif. Score a rectangle of pastel coloured cardboard across the centre and fold it in half to form the card.

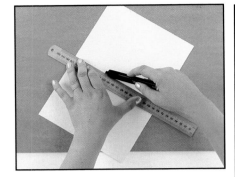

Roughly cut out each picture leaving a margin all round – you will need about seven. Stick them to cartridge paper with spray adhesive; this makes the design easier to cut out. Cut out two complete motifs then cut out the others, discarding more and more of the background with each one. The picture is built up in layers.

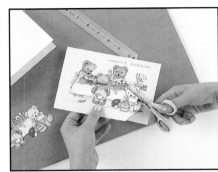

Use spray adhesive to stick one of the complete pictures to the front of the card. Stick double-sided adhesive foam pieces all over the picture. Carefully place the other complete picture on top and press lightly to secure it in place. Add the other layers with foam pieces between until the last smallest detail is in position.

The bouquet on this bright and cheerful greeting card is made up of coloured gummed paper squares torn into simple shapes. Cut a rectangle of white cardboard measuring 38cm x 25cm (15in x 10in). Score across the centre widthwise using a craft knife. Fold the card in half along the scored line.

All the shapes have straight edges. Press a ruler across a gummed square, lift one edge of paper and pull it up against the ruler to tear it neatly. Now tear across the paper again either diagonally or straight across to form the various shapes.

Arrange the pieces on the front of the card within a border of narrow strips and squares. Moisten the back of the gummed pieces to stick them in position.

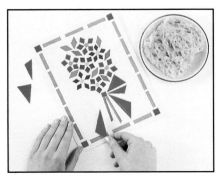

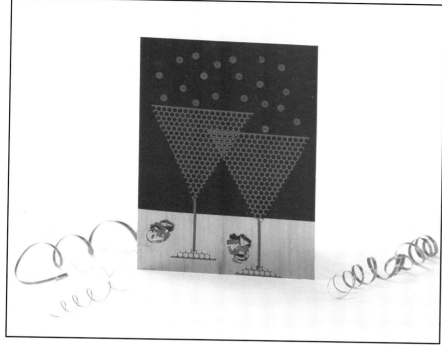

T his card, in a party mood, could be used for a birthday, engagement or congratulations. Cut a glossy purple card 20cm x 30cm (8in x 12in). Score down the centre and fold. Cut two triangular shapes and bases from pink sequin waste and a piece of iridescent film to fit the width of the card. Mark with pencil dots where the glasses should be placed.

A favourite Victorian pastime was to make greeting cards from printed 'scraps'. Cut a piece of cardboard 42cm x 25cm (16½in x 10in) and score across the centre widthwise. Fold the card in half. Cut out a large heart from mottled pink paper and glue it to the middle of the card.

Using spray adhesive, spray glue on to the back of the iridescent 'table' and smooth down on to the card, removing creases. Trim away any excess. Spray glue on to the back of the cocktail glasses and position on dot marks. Spray bases at the same time.

Cut out sprays of flowers from reproductions of sheets of Victorian scraps, available at craft shops and some museums. Alternatively, use pictures from seed catalogues. Arrange the flowers along the edge of the heart and when you are happy with the design glue them in place. Glue on single flowers to fill any gaps in between.

With a rubber-based glue, stick down strips of very narrow ribbon for the stems, then the bases. Curl two narrow pieces of ribbon, and place sequin 'bubbles' over glasses. A pair of tweezers will make this an easier task. Glue curls of ribbon on the 'table' and leave for a few minutes for the glue to set. Any residue may be gently rubbed away when dry.

Highlight the flowers with a fine gold pen. Use a thick gold pen to draw a line 2cm (¾in) from the ends of the card. Cut two 1.5cm (⅝in) wide strips of marbled paper and glue along the ends of the card with spray glue. To finish, stick a butterfly or other motif in one corner.

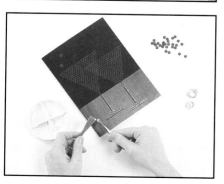

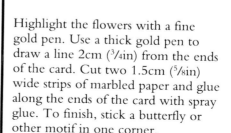

A lively teenage motif badge for sewing on to jeans and jackets makes a card and gift – it can be carefully peeled off the card at a later date and sewn on to a favourite garment. To put the pop singer in the spotlight, cut a glossy red card 15cm x 22cm (6in x 8½in). Score and fold in half. Draw a spotlight shape on silver paper or plastic film using a ruler.

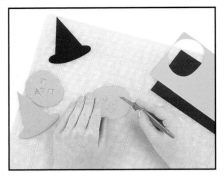

A fun 'spook' for Halloween, quickly and easily made from paper and sequins. Cut red card 22cm x 16cm (8½in x 6¼in). Score and fold 11cm (4¼in). Draw a simple pumpkin face and witch's hat and make your own templates. Cut out the witch's hat from black paper or card. Cut the pumpkin head from orange paper or card, then cut out eyes and mouth.

Cut out the spotlight with a craft knife and trim the curve with a pair of small scissors.

Position the head and hat on the card and mark with a sharp pencil. Glue the pieces in place.

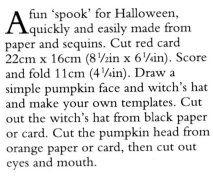

First glue down the spotlight and trim any overhang on the edge of the card. Stick down the pop singer with rubber-based glue and hold firmly in place for a minute or two until the glue dries. The discs on the main picture are buttons purchased from a specialist button shop.

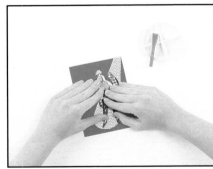

Add sequin stars and moons using rubber-based glue, holding them in place for a moment while the glue dries. Tweezers make handling the sequins easier.

Size up patterns as described on page 25, making each square of your grid measure 3cm (1¼in).

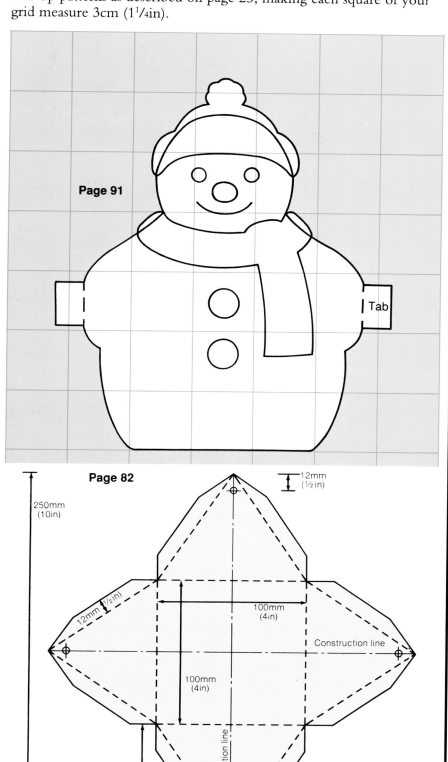

Page 91

Tab

Page 82

250mm
(10in)

12mm
(½in)

12mm (½in)

100mm
(4in)

Construction line

100mm
(4in)

Construction line

75mm
(3in)

50mm
(2in)

50mm
(2in)

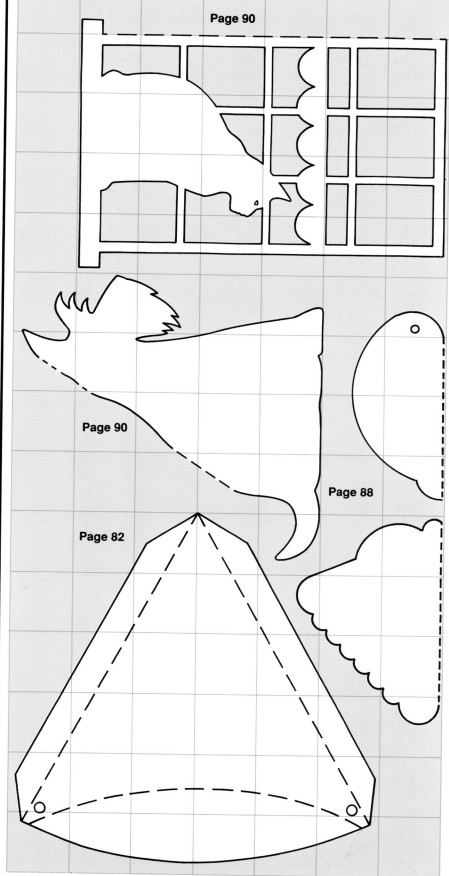

Page 90

Page 90

Page 82

Page 88

INDEX